More Praise for
How Did You Know That?
The Story of a World Renowned Psychic

"I ran many of the Psychic Fairs in Long Island during the 1990's. Joy is the most straightforward psychic I have ever met. She knows the value of sincerity in giving a client a psychic reading. Due to her integrity and no nonsense attitude, she is the most sought after spiritualist I know. Joy is totally honest in her readings, and believes wholeheartedly in her chosen work. Thank you, Joy, for the excellent work you have been doing and will keep on doing. You bring 'Joy' to your clients."
—*Herb Lions Potish*

"Joy is a life changer, the work that Joy does in guiding people is priceless. Blessings and Love."
—*Janet Russell Intuitive/Spiritual Medium*
TV Host and Producer of Janet Russell Presents.com

"When I first met Joy she told me 'your Father watched you working on the furniture and he is very proud of you and he said you did a good job'. I had sanded the rust off the outdoor furniture and repainted it. My Dad, who is deceased, was in the steel business and this would definitely be something he would say and only something I would know. It gave me peace to know he is watching over me. Joy was right on target, she is great."

—*Karen*

"We felt a tremendous loss when Joy, Long Island's leading psychic, no longer worked at our fairs. She had been proven incredibly accurate in her readings, and the fairs definitely suffered enormously without her. She is a wonderful friend, and we miss and love her with all our hearts.

Joy is known to be sincere, honorable and genuine to everyone. Even though she is accustomed to regarding her talent as an everyday, usual event, we consider her a woman with a very special ability. This book depicts her amazing capabilities, and we are thrilled for her!"

—*Mindy and Frank*
The Original Psychic Fair

"I was always somewhat of a skeptic, but that changed when I met Joy. She told me she saw three men around me and named my husband and my one brother. It is when she mentioned my other brother's name and said he was watching over me, that is when I really got the chills. He died when he was 6 and not many people, even some of my family, knew of his existence. I became a believer that day and that was because of Joy."

—*I.G.*

"Your service has been invaluable to my family."

—*Dr. John A.*

"I never believed in psychics but after meeting Joy, I'm hooked. Joy's reading nailed every point and made a huge difference in my life. I hit the psychic jackpot when I discovered Joy and I'm forever grateful for the experience."

—S.I.

"Joy's vision and gift are simply amazing. Joy has been spot on about my dating life and health issues. Joy's psychic readings are wonderful."

—Charlie

"Joy knew the names of all my children and other family members at my initial reading even though she knew absolutely nothing about me. I have to say that her accuracy of predictions has helped guide me through the years. I call Joy my angel from heaven. I just can't THANK her enough!"

—Jaymee

HOW DID YOU KNOW THAT?

The Story of a World Renowned Psychic

JOY IEMMITI
with Natalie Krous

How Did You Know That? The Story of a World Renowned Psychic
Copyright © 2016 Joy Iemmiti with Natalie Krous

Originally published as:
"Blessed With A Joyful Gift: Psychic Moments for You and Me"

All rights reserved. No part of this book may be reproduced (except for inclusion in reviews), disseminated or utilized in any form or by any means, electronic or mechanical, including photocopying, recording, or in any information storage and retrieval system, or the Internet/World Wide Web without written permission from the author or publisher.

Joy Iemmiti's work is for entertainment purposes only
For further information please contact: psychicjoy3@gmail.com

Printed in the United States of America
First Edition Printing

Design by
Arbor Services, Inc.
http://www.arborservices.co/

ISBN: 978-0-692-65962-5
LCCN: 2016903911
1. Title   2. Author   3. Body, Mind, and Spirit

Contents

Acknowledgments	1
Clairvoyant Thinking	3

PART ONE
Can You Hear What I Am Hearing?   7

Chapter One
Family Photo   12

Chapter Two
Moving Along   31

Chapter Three
Scary Times   52

Chapter Four
Volunteering, Jobs and Careers   76

Chapter Five
Taking My Chances   94

Chapter Six
Personal Things   106

PART TWO
Reading for Others   123

Chapter Seven
How Did You Know That?   127

Chapter Eight
Work, Play and More   161

Chapter Nine
Sad to Say (But Sometimes With a Happy Ending)   197

Chapter Ten
This and That   235

Chapter Eleven
She/Her and He/Him   277

Chapter Twelve
A Little Something Extra to Think About   300

THE END…?
Living Our Lives   312

Afterword by Natalie Krous   315

Acknowledgments

God, the supreme being—master of this magical universe, connecting us all.

Max Schneider—you inspired the book's theme and knew it was really so. May you rest in peace.

Natalie Krous—I truly appreciate the contribution of your amazing talents. You bring out the best in others by always giving the very best of yourself. You believed in me, never complained and never gave an excuse for not being able to collaborate. You got involved. What I admire the most about you are your motivation, intelligence and passion for the subject. Thank you, Natalie, for your tireless efforts in helping to make my book a success.

Zach—my understanding husband. Thank you for being such a good sport and allowing these stories to be told. You are the anchor that keeps me grounded.

Grandma Mabel and Grandpa Michael—I am proud of who and where I came from. I love you to the stars!

Mom and Dad—thank you for giving me the life I was born to live. You knew I was different and respected the path that I chose.

Mindy and Frank—it was truly an honor and a privilege to be a reader and clairvoyant at your psychic fairs. I have the greatest admiration for your service. You are an excellent team and I send my very best wishes for your continued success.

Janet—thank you for allowing me to be featured on your television show. It was the opportunity of a lifetime.

Barbara—you taught me that there is meaning in every psychic message.

Lee and Herb—thank you for your continued friendship, encouragement and good wishes.

Joyce and Jack—thank you for inviting me as a frequent guest on your talk-radio show.

Clairvoyant Thinking

My name is Joy Iemmiti and I have messages for you...all of you. But I will only give them to you if you are interested in hearing them.

Yes, I receive valid information and communications from an anonymous source in an unknown place. As a clairvoyant and a tarot card reader who has personally witnessed extraordinary paranormal experiences throughout my entire life, I have developed an additional expertise on the subject after having given thousands and thousands of sensory-oriented readings to others during the last four decades.

Throughout all those years, so many of my friends and clients have asked, "Why don't you write a book?" Well, I did...and here it is. In this volume of numerous anecdotal recollections, you will read a compilation of many of my own personal psychic happenings as well as selected excerpts from mediumistic readings that I've given to others. I'm positive that you will enjoy this record of my telepathic experiences. Why am I so certain? Because, I'm clairvoyant (a little psychic humor.)

Although my resume includes various types of jobs and hobbies, some of which you will read about later in this book, the one I thoroughly focus on and enjoy the most has been and still is, my career in metaphysics. I have shared my abilities and knowledge at psychic fairs, private parties and fundraising charity events and in numerous telephone readings.

This career has given me much exposure to various media outlets. My television experiences include interviews regarding psychic phenomenon and many appearances as the sole clairvoyant of the hour on local cable shows dealing with this subject. I have also had the pleasure of being invited frequently as a guest speaker on talk radio. My resume could not leave out the fact that I was given the honor of being chosen as a featured psychic regarding the subject of metaphysics in articles printed by two prominent New York newspapers.

Why was I chosen to have this skill? I really don't have a grasp of the answer as to why I was given this talent and probably never will but much personal insight is there for me and I eagerly share it with others. The messages that I receive are real, informative and accurate. This knowledge and certainty of clairvoyance which I have been blessed with is something that mystifies many. I probably do not even realize its ultimate magnificence because the psychic ability I possess is something that has been with me since birth. I've always had this gift and subsequently, the resulting outcome has continually been an integral part of my life. To me, it is a natural and expected phenomenon. I view this knowledge as a truly rare and unique capability. Only a few are fortunately privileged to possess it.

If you are interested in the mind and what it is capable of, then you most certainly have chosen the correct book to read. After reading this journal of my skill and possibly finding yourself in awe of the unknown, I urge you to try to open up your own path of clairvoyance. Perhaps the interpretations of these actual written accounts will activate the needed perseverance, turning fascination into confident sought -after results never before dreamed of a possibility. You have the potential to do it-every person does.

I promise that these stories will be an adventure that will keep you thinking and thinking. Do not be afraid or hesitant to do that. Respect your mind and realize its innate abilities.

You might have had the opportunity to meet me during one of my many metaphysical readings, whether it was in my home, at the psychic fair, on the phone, or just as a casual encounter in some long-forgotten place. If I provided you with correct information that hadn't previously been told to me, please think of me as person like yourself-but just with a little twist.

PART ONE

Can You Hear What I Am Hearing?

My parents named me Marilyn and even though I thought it was a nice name, I just wasn't comfortable with it. I preferred my middle name, which is Joy. I substituted my middle name for my first name prior to my entrance to kindergarten. I wouldn't respond to the name Marilyn from anyone, including my parents, teachers and friends. My name was going to be Joy forever!

I discovered my psychic realization very early in life. It came through specific voices speaking to me. Thinking that this was the norm for everyone, I assumed that hearing utterances from unknown places was a way of life for all.

The following is an actual event that I experienced as a young child:

While eating breakfast in the kitchen alone one morning, I began to hear many voices speaking to me, all at the same time. My mother, who was sitting in the living room, watching television, was unaware of this barrage of babble. I hadn't discussed the voices with her, so it was not an issue that she was aware of.

Since the constant chatter was disturbing my meal, I yelled to them, "Be quiet!"

My mother, not knowing what was happening, angrily answered me, "Don't use that tone with me. Who do you think you're talking to? I'm not even saying anything. Are you on the phone?"

I told her that I wasn't speaking to her, nor was I on the telephone. But I continued yelling out to the voices to be quiet.

My mother asked me again who I was shouting at. She inquired if anyone was sitting in the kitchen with me. All of my answers were "no." I then told her that I was speaking to "the voices," thinking that by then, she must have heard them also.

This was the beginning of a lifetime full of voices. Usually it was one voice, but occasionally it was a chorus of talking such as the ones in the kitchen that morning.

It all came together during first grade when my teacher, Mrs. Elkins, started the school year by referring to me as Marilyn. Not willing to tolerate any of that, I just refused to respond. Finally, upon her questioning, I respectfully explained to her that if she wanted an answer from me, she would have to call me by the name of Joy. After agreeing to honor my wish, she realized that I still wasn't responding. Thinking that I was daydreaming, or more likely had a hearing loss, Mrs. Elkins sent me to the school nurse to have my hearing evaluated.

The nurse was not too happy about or impressed by my responses during the test, which was conducted on a sophisticated piece of equipment. A total evaluation of my auditory senses revealed that the assessment results fell short of the parameters for normal hearing. After reviewing the outcome of the examination, she recommended that my mother take me to the family doctor. So, off Mom and I went. We were going to negate or validate my teacher's and the school nurse's suspicions about my sense of hearing.

The doctor, upon examining me, could not find any definitive problem, but to ensure a correct diagnosis decided to send me to a hearing specialist who could perform more elaborate and specific tests regarding the possibility of impairment. So, off Mom and I went again, but this time to the ear, nose and throat doctor.

After the new doctor administered his tests, he decided that the removal of my tonsils was warranted. He explained that this would alleviate the entire problem of a hearing loss, so the decision was made by all who were present that my tonsils would be extracted.

It was then that my mother blurted out, "Joy hears voices, whatever that means."

The doctor turned to me and asked, "Do you have an imaginary friend?"

I looked at him and said, "No." I had no idea what he was talking about.

After he shrugged his shoulders, I could see the look of pity in his eyes. He was thinking that this poor woman had a problem child whom she would have to raise.

How did I know? I could hear the thoughts moving through his mind!

As I grew older and experienced more psychic occurrences, the realization that I could fine tune my people skills came into play. The following is another story of an actual metaphysical happening:

When I graduated to using tarot cards for divination at the age of thirteen, my new friend Cindy, who had recently moved to the neighborhood, persuaded me to give her mom, Mary, a card reading. I had only been studying tarot for ten months, having saved my babysitting money for this special purchase of brand new cards.

As soon as Mary sat down, a familiar energy ignited within me even though it was the first time my tarot cards were being used. I asked Mary not to cross her arms or legs, explaining briefly that the mystical charge I needed could not be blocked. After saying these instructions, I continued my attempt to be very professional and asked her to shuffle the cards. I also requested that she seriously consider what she wanted to be informed about. Mary told me that she wasn't thinking about anything in particular.

After taking a deep breath, I readied myself for my first tarot card reading. Strangely enough, after a few moments, the cards starting speaking to me by communicating what was on Mary's subconscious mind. They told me that she had experienced four pregnancies during her life.

After verbalizing what the cards told me, Cindy, who had been observing all of this rather skeptically, laughed out loud and informed me that I was incorrect. She proudly brought to my attention that she had only one older brother, whom I wasn't aware of. He was away at college.

After briefly pondering Cindy's answer, I explained with much confidence that her mother had suffered two miscarriages before Cindy's birth. There was no doubt in my mind concerning the truth of my reading.

Cindy stopped laughing and suddenly became serious. My new friend looked to her mother for substantiation of my tarot card reading or the facts that Cindy had just finished telling me.

Mary wiped her eyes with a handkerchief that she was holding. She didn't confirm my reading or voice any objection to its validity. Instead, she said to me with genuine, deep emotion in her voice, "God gave you a special gift." I then knew that my first tarot card reading was correct.

This, my initial tarot card experience given to a stranger, was a short but meaningful one. It taught me that people can be very private, perhaps not wanting to discuss certain actions and sensitive subjects. It also warned me to be careful how I interpret the cards because they truly do not lie and must be read correctly!

Chapter One

Family Photo

One of my first recollections regarding the sensory messages of psychic ability goes back to the time when I was five years old. At that point in my life, my favorite pastime was playing with dolls, a passion that many little girls that age have.

But there was one particular doll I truly loved. Her name was Louise. She was my favorite, and I treated her as such by tenderly caring for her as though she were a real baby. This meant dressing her every day and pretending to feed and nurture her as though she were an actual person.

One evening before going to bed with my baby Louise, I suddenly felt a fear invade me. A warning voice said that my doll would have to be safeguarded that night. I looked for a helmet, hat or umbrella—something that meant protection to me. Not being able to find what suited my needs, without anyone's knowledge, I left my bed, walked to the refrigerator and opened the door. I placed Louise inside, all the way in the back, thinking that this was the safest place for her. After closing the door, I quietly tiptoed back to bed, slid under the covers and fell quickly to sleep.

Shortly after waking from a restful slumber that same night, a realization struck me that I had no idea where I was or who I was with. While lying on a couch in an unfamiliar room with a stranger, a middle-aged woman watching me,

I found myself in an unusual situation. My memory of that incident is that of being confused but not scared. In fact, there was a feeling of safety and security. I questioned the woman sitting next to me in regard to the safety of my family. She was startled. How did I know about the fire?

The story that she relayed to me wasn't really a surprise. She explained that while I was in a deep sleep, my father carried me next door to our neighbor's house, which was the one I was currently in. He asked this woman, who was the babysitter, if he could leave me there until the fire, which had started in our living room television set, was under control.

This event happened in the middle of winter and I slept through the entire incident, even though my father rushed me out of the house so quickly that a coat wasn't even put on me. The babysitter continued her story, telling me that I was actually next door to my own house. I had never been in this house before that evening because two boys lived there and they were not playmates of mine.

The next morning, my father came to the house and after graciously thanking the neighbors for taking care of his daughter, brought me home. In its own way, it was a fun night because I was always one who looked for adventures that, of course, were safe ones.

Upon returning home, I immediately walked to the refrigerator to remove my little doll, Louise. My mother, who frowned upon my going to the refrigerator without asking, saw me take her out. She asked, "Why is your doll in there?"

I explained to her that I didn't want my baby to be hurt. Innocently revealing the ominous warning that was imparted to me the night before, I kissed my newly retrieved Louise. My mother stood there stunned. She was absolutely dumbfounded. Even to this day, I think about the puzzled look on her face.

Entry level for me?

As you can see from the last story, my doll Louise was something very special to me. All my friends living on the block knew how much I loved her. Even though they were equally fond of their own dolls, my hope was that they knew that Louise was exceptional.

One Sunday, before going to church, I decided to place Louise outside in the backyard to get some fresh air because she was confined to my bedroom so much of the time. The reasoning behind my actions concerned the rationale that even dolls needed fresh air.

On that particular day, I clothed her in a white dress with a red bow that my Grandma Mabel had made for her. So that she wouldn't be cold, I added a sweater with pearl buttons, which was also one of my grandma's creations. After getting Louise ready for the day and assessing how she looked, as any mother would do, I was content that my maternal instinct had been fulfilled. It gave me pride to see her in her Sunday best.

I then brought her into the yard and positioned her so that she could enjoy the bright sunshine of a lovely day. After propping her up in a lawn chair, thinking that she would be safe, my feeling was that the morning was going to be starting off with contentment and satisfaction.

My parents and I went to church, making it a typical Sunday morning except for the fact that Louise was out on the patio. I thought about my precious doll and missed her during the services, but at the same time knew that she would be waiting for me when our car pulled into the driveway later that day.

After church, my father stopped at the local bakery to get some bread for us and I stayed in the car with my mother, waiting for him. Suddenly, a picture started forming in my mind's eye, showing me that my friend Roberta had come to my house looking for me. After going into the backyard, thinking that I might be there, she saw Louise and took her. I shouted to my mother, "Momma, Momma, my doll is being kidnapped." My mother, not understanding what I was yelling about, told me to stop shouting, saying that we would be home soon.

Upon arriving home, I ran directly to the yard and, confirming my vision, Louise was gone. My suspicions had been real. After informing my mother that I was going to Roberta's house to retrieve my doll, my mother cautioned me not to go by saying that a person can't just accuse someone else of something without proof.

Considering that there were at least twelve girls on the block whom I played with, normally it would have been a good point. But I told her that I was sure that the kidnapper was Roberta. Refusing to listen to my mother's advice because I had seen the picture of the theft in my mind, I readied myself for a confrontation with my soon-to-be ex-friend. Talk about eyes. My poor mother's eyes rolled. She could not convince me not to go and accuse Roberta of stealing my little Louise.

Running down the block only intensified my panic regarding the doll's disappearance. Soon I found myself knocking on the door of Roberta's house. Her mother, Mrs. Blair, answered the door. When I asked to see Roberta, she informed me that my friend couldn't come out now because she was eating her lunch.

I told Mrs. Blair that Roberta had taken my doll, Louise, and that I wanted her back. Mrs. Blair shouted to Roberta, who was in the kitchen, asking her if she had possession of my doll. It was at that point that Roberta came to the door and vehemently denied having taken Louise.

I became furious and, without waiting to be invited inside, defiantly pushed my way into the hallway, rushed past both of them and walked resolutely up the steps to Roberta's room, followed by mother and daughter. I found Louise sitting amongst many other dolls in the room. After pointing to my baby, thus showing Mrs. Blair and Roberta my precious toy still dressed in the clothing my grandmother had made for her, I waited to see their reactions. Apparently, not knowing what to say, Roberta stuttered that she didn't know that she had her. She then stammered that she must have taken Louise by accident.

Her mother, who was embarrassed and angry, had no problem telling Roberta there would be a punishment not only for stealing something but also for lying about it. My relationship with Roberta ended for a long period of time after that incident.

Years later, when we were teenagers, the friendship was renewed. Roberta apologized for the theft but said that she was curious as to how I knew she was the culprit. Roberta was sure that I had visually seen her take the toy. I explained to her that I just knew. This answer did not satisfy her, so she asked me if I had knocked on the doors of all the girls on the block who were my playmates, asking them if they had taken Louise. Again, my answer was "no." I simply said that my mind's eye showed her taking Louise and there were no doubts about it. She never understood my response and continued to ask me for years after the incident how I arrived at this conclusion.

It was a happening that I now assume was just a childhood fascination having to do with wanting someone else's toy and actually acting on it. If I hadn't seen it in my mind, I never could have determined which of my friends actually took my beloved doll.

Thank goodness for mother's intuition!

Here is a story that many of you can possibly relate to from your youth.

It was summertime and every single day, my mother would make me eat the same thing for lunch. This would be an alright situation except that the food that she gave me was something that I despised eating. What was it? Cream cheese and jelly on white bread.

When I complained to her by saying how I disliked the taste of it, she lectured me about all the starving children in Africa. (How many of you have heard that one?) With that, Mom would make me sit at the kitchen table and eat it until every last morsel was gone. She watched over me the way a guard would watch over a prisoner. (Where were my mystical powers when I needed them?)

I decided to become creative to get out of this situation, so since the weather was warm, I asked permission to eat outside at the picnic table located on the patio in the backyard. Thankfully, my mother was in agreement with me because there would be no mess for her to clean up in the kitchen. My mother was a very fastidious person as well as a perfectionist and always believed that the notion of cleanliness ranked highest in importance when compared to any activity.

Now, I was sent into the backyard to eat my lunch. Since the bushes in the rear yard were full during the summertime, I realized that there was the possibility of hiding my sandwiches in them. No one would ever know. Since I wasn't in my mom's view and therefore not being watched, she wouldn't be any wiser concerning my lunch. So, every afternoon, I buried the contents of my plate in the green shrubbery and then proceeded into the house to show my mother that every speck of food had been eaten off the now-empty plate. This proved that I had fulfilled her wishes regarding my luncheon meal each day. It was working out very well and the rest of the summer passed uneventfully.

Soon, the fall season arrived. My mind was filled with school challenges, meeting new friends and other issues that occupy the days of any young child. I had forgotten about my summer deed of disposing the cream cheese and jelly sandwiches.

One day in early October, I was told that my mother's cousins, Yvonne and Peter, were coming to visit us. Now, normally, this would have been an exciting piece of information, but from the moment that I was told of the impending visit, an intimidating feeling invaded my being. For some reason not yet known to me, I was going to be in trouble—big trouble. In my mind's eye, there was Mom wagging her finger at me. I became very fearful without knowing why, but as usual, it made sense that the reason would show itself soon enough.

That day arrived and so did the expected company. My mom suggested to her guests that they all go out on the patio. I still wasn't thinking about the summer lunch sandwiches and went to the back door to eavesdrop and hear what they were saying.

Yvonne was asking my mother why there were sandwiches in the shrubbery. Since it was autumn, much of the foliage had come off the bushes and the sandwiches were sitting on the little branches, exposed for any observer to see.

Have you ever seen an angry mother? It doesn't compare to the fury that my mother showed me due to my original way of ridding my plate of its food. Now I really had to get imaginative, but my excuse of feeding the birds wasn't exactly working and my punishment, I thought, wasn't really fitting the crime.

That was the end of my outdoor lunches. From then on, every summer I had to eat in the kitchen and sit at the table if it took all day to finish my meal of cream cheese and jelly on white bread.

You know what? To this day, I still hate cream cheese and jelly!

One weekend, my mother asked my father if he would go to the bakery for a loaf of bread. Overhearing her speaking with him, I came into the kitchen and asked her if Daddy could also buy a nine-layer cake.

"What is a nine-layer cake?" she inquired.

"A nine-layer cake is nine layers of cake separated by frosting," I replied. "I can see the cake in the bakery window." Of course, I was viewing it in my psychic vision.

"Joy, I think you mean a seven-layer cake. There is no such thing as a nine-layer cake," my mother replied.

"No, Momma," I protested. "This is nine layers. I can see it."

Of course, my mother, thinking that it was starting to sound tempting, asked my father to bring home a seven-layer cake if the bakery had one. She sent him on his way, telling me again that there was no such thing as a nine-layer cake. Mom finished off the subject by saying that even if I were standing in front of it, the amount of layers would be impossible to determine because there was frosting on the outside of it.

A half hour later, my father came home with the bread and the much-awaited cake. The three of us sat down and devoured our meal with the delicious dessert in mind while we ate.

After dinner, my mother took the cake out of its box and placed it carefully on the table. It was covered in chocolate icing and my taste buds were ready to receive a mouthful of it. I didn't need psychic ability to know that this was going to be a treat. Mom took the knife from the drawer and carefully cut into the brown-chocolate mound sitting on the table.

Suddenly, I heard her give out a laughing scream. She looked at me as if she had seen a bug crawl out of the cake. I ran to look at what caused this outburst from her and there it was: nine layers of cake. My mother was hysterically laughing.

The following week, I went with both my parents to the bakery. I listened while my mother told the woman behind the counter, "My husband bought a nine-layer cake last week and it was delicious. We are back here to buy another one."

"There is no such thing as a nine-layer cake in this bakery. You mean a seven-layer cake," the woman answered. "Believe me, I would know. My name is Gretchen and I am the owner and do the baking. I never make nine-layer cakes."

Again, my mother explained to Gretchen the story regarding the purchase from the previous week. "It was definitely purchased from this store and it was without a doubt nine layers." My father stood there, nodding his head in agreement.

Gretchen sighed in exasperation. She then took out a cake from the bakery showcase, similar to the one purchased by my father the previous week, and placed it on top of the glass counter. She asked my mother for permission to cut into this cake, which, she assumed, we were buying. My mother, anxious to prove the point that it was a nine-layer cake, told the owner of the shop, who was now laughing, that she certainly could.

After carefully cutting a small slice, both women counted the layers. There were only seven.

"See?" the owner said. "There are only seven layers." Then, with a giggle, she said, "I would have charged you extra for the two other layers if I had known about it."

Who said you can't get too much of a good thing?

My Grandma Mabel was very dear to me. She was the kind of typical grandma who babysat, told stories and gave that extra love that every child remembers with happiness.

A story I remember very vividly concerns a psychic vision of mine that occurred while my parents were driving me to my grandmother's house for babysitting purposes. I saw myself drinking cup after cup of hot water. Grandma had never given me hot water to drink but for some reason, I saw myself devouring numerous cups of the liquid.

While sitting in the car on the way to Grandma's house, I asked my mother to tell Grandma not to give me any hot water to drink. My mother looked at me and said, "Why would Grandma Mabel give you hot water to drink? She has other beverages for you." My mother had no clue what I was talking about. Come to think of it, I didn't either.

When we arrived at Grandma Mabel's house, my parents left me in her care and went to do their planned errands. I wondered what we would do because Grandma always had something planned. Maybe we would color with the crayons she kept in the house just for me, or there was the possibility that we could do one of the puzzles that were also left there for my visits with her. Sometimes we baked cookies and sometimes we just talked. It was always a surprise.

After my parents left, Grandma sat me at the dining room table to do a puzzle. She put out a crystal candy dish filled with hard candy. There were all different colors, and she told me to take one. Since green was my favorite color, I chose a lime-flavored one. While doing the puzzle, I started to speak and suddenly, the candy slid down my throat and I began to choke.

Grandma tried to dislodge it with her finger but was of little help. I was so scared. In desperation, she applied pressure on my back. That, too, was unsuccessful. Now I was crying because breathing was becoming difficult and the thought and fear of dying had suddenly entered into my mind.

Just then, Grandma ran into the kitchen and quickly reappeared in front of me with a cup of hot water to drink in order to dissolve the candy. I drank cup after cup and finally, after what seemed like an eternity, the hard candy went down and I was alright.

My grandmother was so upset and nervous that she asked me not to tell my mother about the incident. I gave her my word that I wouldn't.

While riding home, my mother, with a laugh, asked if my grandmother had given me any hot water to drink. I told her that she didn't give me any hot water because if I told her "yes," my mother would wonder why and I didn't want to break my promise to Grandma.

Since that incident, I have never put a hard candy or a lozenge in my mouth. The thought of it brings back the memory of that frightening day!

Are you ready for another Grandma Mabel story? I have so many of them and they are all so precious to me. I loved my grandfather also, but my grandma was especially astute and honest. I remember her as a little lady with gray hair pulled back into a bun, blue eyes and a beautiful smile, and always wearing a hat when she was outdoors. Let's not forget the lace handkerchief, white pearls and sweater with a pocket to hold the handkerchief. (She said that it was ladylike to carry this kind of clothing accessory.)

To me, my grandma was beautiful inside and out. My friends knew that on the Sundays when my grandparents, Mabel and Michael, were coming to visit, I wanted to spend the day with my family. I looked forward to using my babysitting money to buy fruit cocktail and applesauce for Grandma and Grandpa to take home. Although they wanted to pay me, I wouldn't take any money for these treats because it was my pleasure to buy these simple indulgences for them.

Grandma and I would sit and talk with one another for hours. She taught me a lot about life. There is a lot to be said about the elderly. They are the ones with experience and wisdom. She gave me the best advice and even today, I pass it on to young people. Grandma Mabel told me to enjoy being young for as long as possible because childhood goes too quickly. Some of my first profound psychic visions came through her to me, as you will shortly read.

One Sunday, my grandparents came to my house for a visit. Grandma sat down on the sofa, as she always did, and began telling my mother about all the latest family news and stories that were relevant (or irrelevant) to Grandma's life. She finished off the last piece of chitchat by saying, "I am so upset because my favorite lace doily is missing."

While wringing her hands, she continued telling the story: "I kept it on my bedroom dresser and I don't know where it disappeared to." She finished by saying, "Pop even moved the furniture away from the wall so I could see if it fell behind, onto the floor."

As she was relating the story to my mother, a picture started forming in my mind's eye. It was showing me that the doily was in the second drawer of the bedroom dresser in her house, underneath her flannel nightgowns. Of course, since I was seeing it psychically, it meant that there were no doubts about it. Excitedly, I told Grandma where it was. She listened to me and then after thinking about it, disagreed. "I wouldn't have put it in there," she said. But I told Grandma that it was definitely in the drawer and that it was put there accidentally.

When Grandma returned home that day, she called me on the telephone and said, "Joy, you are a real detective because the doily was just where you said it was." She told me that it had gotten caught on the button of one of her nightgowns. When she was putting her laundry away, she had inadvertently grabbed it without noticing that it was being placed in the drawer along with the garment.

You see, revelations are for grandmas too!

Another Grandma Mabel story took place one afternoon when I was a young teenager. I was sitting with her and we were talking about the family tree. I enjoyed hearing the stories about her childhood because it was so far removed from the time and events of my youth.

Suddenly, the name Lillian resounded very loudly in my ear. I had to find out why this name was being given to me, so I asked, "Grandma, who is Lillian?"

She looked at me in a puzzled way and then became very emotional. After grabbing my hand and wiping a tear from her eye, she explained that Lillian was actually her first name. A sister, who was born before her but died shortly thereafter, had the same name but the first and middle names were reversed in order.

I remember thinking to myself, *Boy this is really cool. I actually guessed Grandma's first name.* On that day, my first realization had occurred; it was the precursor of a long career of feeling and hearing the names of people who are deceased, here now and yet to be born.

I am sometimes able to name the names of members of whole families, whether these people are popular or not within the family!

An example of my fascination with dates concerned October twenty-third. This was the common birthday of both my mother and father. On this date one year, a very strange feeling came over me. I felt that this was going to be the last birthday that would be happily celebrated by both of my parents, but at the same time I did not feel death for either one of them.

I believed that my loving grandma Mabel's life would end on that day the following year. My efforts were futile in trying to shake that premonition. No matter how much of an effort was made to rationalize the fact away, the thought kept coming back to me. It was ridiculous. How could I predict something that was going to happen one year from then? She wasn't even ill. I wouldn't dare express this troubling hunch to anyone.

The following October twenty-third, my grandma was in a nursing home and my parents wanted to skip that visiting day because they wanted to celebrate their mutual birthday. When they told me that they weren't going to see Grandma, I should have told them that this was their last chance to see her alive, but I thought that maybe—hopefully—I was wrong. To this day, I regret not warning them. In reality, my reticence regarding the disclosure of this information was due to the fact that they would think that I was delusional, telling them that I was aware of the exact day Grandma was going to die.

Unfortunately, her death came to pass that day and actually, it frightened me that I had this premonition and knowledge. Now, you ask me, how did I know? The previous year, when the message had been shown to me about Grandma's death, I saw it in my mind's eye on a calendar with the date circled. How did I know it was Grandma who was going to die? I don't know how. I just felt it in my heart!

Years later, my husband, Zach, took me to the cemetery to visit my grandma's grave. It was late in the day and I was happy to be there because I hadn't visited the grave since her funeral, which had taken place a number of years before. The reason why there were no follow-up visits was because I don't place that much importance on visiting graves. My feelings on the subject are that deeds for the living are what count. What you do for the deceased you do for yourself.

There were hundreds and hundreds of graves and I couldn't remember exactly where she was buried. The office of the cemetery was closed and I had no frame of reference or map to guide me. The last time I had been there was the day she was buried, and it had been a very emotional time for me. Having no recollection except for the name of the cemetery in which she was interred left me with a difficult task at hand. Where was Grandma Mabel?

We walked up and down all the rows for hours. Finally, after many false leads, we decided to leave. As we turned to go, a little voice in my head whispered, "Turn around and walk straight." We did. It led us right to her grave site. I said, "Grandma, this is Zach. I wish you could have met him, but someday you will."

Guess who guided me to the grave. My anonymous source really helped me out that day!

When I was in the sixth grade, similar to many other girls my age, I was eager to be grown up, act grown up and look grown up. So, when Mom decided that she needed a new handbag and then bought one, I respectfully asked for permission to retrieve her old one from the pile of old clothes and goods. It was currently being stored in the garage along with other items to be discarded eventually. My mother said that it was not an appropriate purse for someone my age but agreed to give it to me because she was either going to give it away or throw it out anyway.

In retrospect, I now concur with her because the satchel was far too matronly for a young girl and definitely looked like an item that only an older woman would wear. But at that time and at that age, I was happy to look older and was totally thrilled with this new addition to my wardrobe.

I was in possession of this handbag for about one week when my mom informed me that it was time to go shopping for some school clothes. She told me to select an afternoon in which I had little homework.

We went to the local store with my mom driving the family car. While sitting next to her in the passenger seat, a warning psychic vision came to me, saying that Mom's purse was going to be stolen. Upon telling her my newest prophesy, she dismissed it with a laugh, saying that I was being silly to think that she would ever be so careless with her newly purchased bag.

Not willing to treat my latest metaphysical message so haphazardly, I made a mental note to myself to watch her purse carefully while we were shopping. Meanwhile, I held my new purse close to me with all the pride of an adult who had acquired the latest fashion trend.

After entering the store, I watched her handbag continuously; I did not take my eyes off of it. I knew that this was an incident waiting to happen. There were times during this excursion when she trustingly placed the bag on a nearby shelf while she held the potential clothing buy up to my body to see if it would fit. I didn't care about the new clothes because my mind was not focused on that; it was centered on the security of Mom's new leather clutch, which I was concentrating on with my eyes. It was for this reason that anyone within close range of my mom was greeted by a suspicious stare.

At the point in our shopping spree when we had finished with our evaluation of which clothing to buy, I turned around to retrieve my own purse. It was then that I realized that someone had stolen it. Unfortunately, I was so engrossed in Mom's handbag that I neglected to watch my own, which was of course the one that had previously been owned by my mother. Whoever took it probably thought that it belonged to an adult and therefore held valuable contents, including a wallet. Fortunately, it only contained a comb, a mirror, tissues and a pack of gum.

The thief thought that it was "in the bag," but it wasn't!

Chapter Two

Moving Along

Let's go back in time to when I was eight years old. It was a Friday afternoon and my teacher, Mrs. Simpson, made an unexpected announcement, telling the class that the entire third grade would soon be going to a well-known amusement park.

Needless to say, all the students in the grade were very excited to participate in this outing. The time from the afternoon of the disclosure of the trip till the actual day of the event seemed to take forever. All my friends spoke about the upcoming venture during class as well as after the school day ended, while walking home.

The morning of the class excursion finally did arrive, and I waited at the curb along with the rest of my friends, anxious to board the bus in anticipation of a day full of fun. My classmates were ready to sing a multitude of appropriate songs as well as participate in whatever other delightful activities would happen under those circumstances.

Then, just as we were about to enter the big, yellow vehicle, Mrs. Simpson announced that we were allowed to sit in any seat we wished. This, of course, gave us the power to find the best locations with, of course, the most scenic window views. We each climbed up the steps onto the bus and after exploring all of our options fully, settled in for the ride. There were no seat belts or laws regarding this type of safety procedure in place during those days.

The busses carrying all the students in the third grade drove away from the school all in a row, as planned. At that point, for some reason, I suddenly didn't desire or plan to be involved in any happy things that day because there was something disturbing in my thoughts regarding the bus in which I was sitting. The amusement park, which was at least an hour away from our starting point, had suddenly become not that important to me.

I was starting truly to feel the need for safety protection and decided that my current seat would not do. So, after looking around, I quickly spotted a potential new place to sit, which was located in the back of the bus. I hurriedly walked down the aisle and slipped into it, assuming a position with my head between my knees to shield my face. I sat in this position for what seemed to be about ten minutes, but this seat was not alleviating my anxiety either.

For some reason, I couldn't relax and join the fun and the laughter. I knew that the answer to my problem was to get off the bus. Knowing that my vacating the vehicle wasn't going to happen, I decided to change my choice of seating again. The new place being eyed by me was a vacant one in the very front of the bus. I quickly moved into it, but again, there was no relief from my apprehension. After deciding to change my seat again, I noticed an empty one next to the emergency exit, which seemed at that moment to be the perfect spot. It was ideal because it would allow a quick departure when needed.

The feeling of an impending problem was getting stronger and stronger. I felt my heart racing and my anxiety heightening.

My palms became sweaty and my stomach started to hurt. Again, I assumed the position with my head between my knees and waited.

Mrs. Simpson, who, unbeknownst to me, had been watching my movements of switching seats, got up from where she was seated. She walked over to me and said in a tone of voice that was saved for occasions such as this, "Joy, sit still and stop changing your seat. Why is your head between your knees? Do you feel alright?"

It was then that I divulged to her that I needed to find the safest place to sit because the bus was going to be in an accident. She answered me by saying, "The bus will have an accident if you keep moving around and distracting the driver's eyes from the road."

Mrs. Simpson then made an announcement that as of that moment, no one was allowed to move from where he or she was sitting. The place each student was seated in was the one that would be kept for the rest of the trip.

Hopefully, this latest spot that I had picked would suffice, because I had no further choices. My classmates, who all seemed content in their originally chosen seats, did not appear to be disturbed by Mrs. Simpson's statement.

It's important for me to tell you now that this was not the norm for me. Having been a well-behaved child, there was never a need to chastise me regarding the obeying of rules. Never deviating from the expected conduct codes, I respected authority and always did what any well-disciplined child would do.

A half hour later, my premonition came to pass. The bus I was on rear-ended the one in front of it, which was carrying children from another class. The police were called and the trip was delayed for quite a while as a paper report regarding the accident was filled out. There were injuries. Fortunately, they were minor.

Contrary to many beliefs, teachers are only human and they don't know everything!

It was Christmas Day and I was totally thrilled because my gift was a brand-new bicycle. Being twelve years old and never having owned my own bike, it was a gift that thrilled me beyond words. Of course, living in New York and receiving such a present was difficult because it wasn't exactly bike-riding weather during the month of December.

Vowing to be patient until springtime, I continued living my life without the advantages of this type of transportation for afterschool and weekend activities. It just gave me one more thing to look forward to while waiting for the warmer weather to come forth.

Fast forward to the month of April and my friends and I were walking home from school while talking about what activities to do that afternoon. My friend Nancy suggested that we all go for a bike ride. No one had to ask me twice because this was the day I had been waiting for. The winter was gone and the weather was perfect for the trial of my new vehicle. I couldn't wait to reach home in order to change into appropriate bike-riding clothes.

But suddenly, a picture began developing in my psychic vision, showing me that my new bicycle was not in the garage where I had stored it four months earlier. Had the house been robbed? My heart began to beat rapidly and I began to sweat profusely.

I sprinted home, telling my friends before I left them that I needed to do something for my mother before I went bike riding. Arriving at my house, I quickly unlocked the door and ran through all the rooms to the garage, even though I knew that my prized possession was now gone. Fearfully, I looked and as my message had previously shown me, there was no bicycle sitting against the back wall, where it had been stored.

After phoning my friend Nancy and telling her that my bike had been stolen, I waited anxiously, continuously pacing, for my mother to arrive home from work. Unfortunately, there wasn't any way to reach her (no cell phones at that time) because I knew she was en route to the house.

When I saw the family car enter the driveway, I ran as fast as I could to tell her the bad news concerning the robbery. My previous floor pacing had worked me into an emotional state of hysteria.

"Someone stole my bike! It's gone," was my greeting to her that afternoon.

"Nobody stole it. Daddy sold it to someone at work whose daughter is several years younger than you are and wanted a bicycle for her birthday. The man couldn't afford to buy one, so Daddy sold him yours for ten dollars. I was hoping that you wouldn't notice that it was gone or maybe wouldn't care to ride a bike anymore," my mother's answered.

I remember standing there in a state of bewilderment. My mind was racing, looking for an answer to give to this woman, my mother, regarding the fate of my bicycle. What about me?

Was my father more interested in a stranger than he was in his own daughter? I vacillated from anger to compassion for this little girl who also wanted a bike. Where was the pity for me?

Hours later, when my father came home from work, I was waiting with a whole story for him regarding my Christmas gift. As he walked through the door, I ran to him, carrying the emotional agony that had been raging in me the entire afternoon.

"Mommy told me that you sold my new bike," I cried to him. "How could you do that to me? You didn't even tell me." I stood in front of him, letting all my pent-up emotions from that day flow.

"What do you mean?" he answered. "You never ride it."

"How could I ride it during the winter? It's too cold and there is always snow on the ground." I couldn't believe how unfair this was. While sobbing, I told him how unhappy I was to have this Christmas gift of a long-awaited bicycle taken away from me.

"Listen, Joy," he said, "sometimes you have to have some feelings for other people. This little girl wanted a bicycle also and her father couldn't afford it. It is a very sad story and I felt very badly for her father. I thought that you wouldn't care."

Looking back at the event, I feel both anger and pride regarding my father. Had it been a message to and perhaps a lesson for me when I saw the vision of my missing bicycle? It probably was, but it was a very painful one.

It's hard to be a kid!

Fast forward to many years later when a group of my friends asked me if I would be interested in traveling with them across the United States by car. They reasoned that it would be a relatively inexpensive way to see the country, journeying the northern route going west and returning via the southern states going east. Our goal was to see as much scenery as possible.

It sounded like a fun adventure and I was enthused to go. Of course, there was the chance that the car would break down or we would be stranded anywhere in this vast nation, but I thought that there were enough of us going that it would be relatively safe.

We left New York and had an uneventful beginning of the trip as we enjoyed our freedom as well as the luscious landscape comprised of more greenery than we had ever envisioned. All of us were satisfied that the correct decision had been made regarding the trip.

As soon as we attained our goal of reaching the West Coast, we planned for our adventurous trek going eastward. After studying the map, many discussions were undertaken and proposals were made, and finally we all agreed upon the planned highlights of the journey back to New York. With a definite purpose in mind, the itinerary was in place for the trip home, which focused on taking the southern route as originally planned.

Our homeward-bound part of the vacation began and all of its objectives were going smoothly until one particular afternoon. Suddenly, while traveling, I had a foreboding sense of fear. There was a profoundly frightening disaster on its way. I wasn't sure what it was, but I knew that it was going to happen that day, and it was going to be life-threatening. The danger felt catastrophic.

Because the negative instinct I was feeling was so intense, it was decided by all of us that it would be prudent to stop at a local gas station to have the car examined for any potential problems. Even though there was going to be a fee for this service, it was certainly logical to ask the mechanic to check the entire car in order to allay any apprehension regarding the long ride that lay ahead of us.

After viewing the motor, tires and whatever else mechanics look at, he told us that the automobile and its parts looked fine to him and gave us a thumbs-up sign, which satisfied everyone except me. The trip continued, as did my anxiety.

Eventually, one of my fellow travelers, who trusted my intuitive skills and respected my continuing negative premonition, turned to me as tears rolled down her cheeks. "Are we going to be alright?"

I told her that the feeling was still there, but I could not pinpoint the problem. Perhaps I would eventually hear the voice or see the picture in my mind but as of that moment, all I had was the feeling.

As our automobile entered the state of New Mexico, my heart started racing with such intensity that my friend who was driving had to pull in to a shopping center until I calmed down or felt that we were no longer in danger. We sat there for approximately one hour when suddenly we realized that all the vehicles traveling in the same direction our car had been going previously were being turned around. Surprisingly, there were roadblocks and state troopers surrounding us. We all exited our car to find out what the problem was.

The officer to whom we made the inquiry told us that the road was closed because of mud slides. There were rocks falling from the tops of the mountains and hitting cars, resulting in numerous accidents and injuries. He said, "Anyone who would have been on that winding road one hour ago would have been killed."

It was strange that I didn't see the problem in my mind or hear the warning in my ear. It was just a feeling that would not let go of me.

Psychic abilities are portable. They can move across the country and back and don't need to be packed in a suitcase!

Car racing was something that was very different for me. It seemed exhilarating and exciting. Even though I began to take an interest in the sport as a spectator, as time went by, I was tempted to become more involved.

One day, a friend of mine dared me to become a participant instead of an observer. I took that dare. I knew of the possible danger, but the love of challenges and thrills enticed me to try it. My feeling was that if I were careful and took every logical precaution, there would no problems.

Every week, when putting on my helmet and fireproof jumpsuit, an invigorating feeling permeated my being and I would excitedly get behind the wheel and zoom. I was off like a real daredevil!

One Saturday afternoon, I was talking to another driver whose name was Phil. He was getting ready for his race and was very confident even though he had slightly more experience than I did. As I spoke with him before his race, a little voice in my head told me that this was going to be his last race. Hoping he would listen to me, I relayed to Phil that I had a bad feeling about him racing that afternoon. Without telling him anything specific, I just tried to convince him that he should be an onlooker instead of a driver that particular day. He refused to listen.

While racing, he lost control of the car and crashed head on into a cement wall. It was one of the worse sights I have ever seen in my life.

I didn't know Phil except for the brief encounter with him earlier that day before the race, but nevertheless, I felt responsible for the accident and subsequently took the trip to the emergency room of the local hospital to where he had been brought. Having seen the incident coming and having not tried to prevent it in a stronger manner gave me tremendous guilt. As I entered the hospital to inquire about his condition, his screams due to the pain he was experiencing echoed throughout the entire floor. I stood there crying and blaming myself for the accident's occurrence. Unfortunately, due to his massive injuries, he ultimately lost a great deal of blood and died that afternoon.

People think that a psychic gift is always fun. Believe me, it's not!

Moving Along

One Sunday, in between client readings, I decided to give my husband, Zach, a tarot card reading. When I asked him what he would like the cards to tell him about, he thought about it briefly and then asked me to tell him what was in store for his business during the upcoming week.

I put the cards out and was quite distressed at what they showed. The reading was telling me that within in the next few days, Zach's business would be robbed.

On the following Wednesday, Zach phoned me from work, obviously stressed and upset. When I asked him what was wrong, he told me that his truck had been sitting in the front of the building with the motor running. The vehicle was loaded to capacity because he was about to make a delivery of goods. As he was ready to leave, Zach realized that he had neglected to bring his eyeglasses with him. They were on top of his desk in the office. While still allowing the motor of the tractor trailer to run, he went back into the building to get them.

When he returned, the fully loaded truck was gone. When I reminded him of the tarot reading earlier in the week, warning him that he was going to be robbed at work, he told me that had totally forgotten about it. Zach added to his defense of not being more careful after the ominous prediction that he had just assumed that it was going to be cash and not his tractor trailer filled to the brim with inventory.

Hello…a truck and its merchandise is money too!

During one winter, an organization that Zach and I belonged to sponsored a weekend getaway at a Pennsylvania resort. I looked forward to going and didn't anticipate a problem at the time. Zach, who was quite an athlete and an avid skier, was very proud of his expertise in the area of sports. I personally was not someone who enjoyed this type of activity, especially since it involved heights.

We arrived there Friday night, enjoyed a nice dinner and relaxed in anticipation of a fun-filled weekend. It was a good choice for an escape from our daily routine.

On Saturday morning, upon waking, a vision suddenly started to unfold in my mind's eye. I was viewing Zach on crutches due to a broken right leg. The mental image also showed me that I was going to have to drive home (a several-hour ride) from this resort.

After telling him about my visualization of a soon-to-be event, he claimed that I was being too much of a worrier. Zach assured me that he was an expert skier and suggested that I should just sit in the lobby and wait for him. He then left to start his day on the slopes.

An hour later, I heard a commotion coming from outside the ski lodge. Curious as to what all the activity was about, I wandered over to look out the door. Shortly afterwards, an ambulance became visible in the distance. No one even had to tell me what the problem was. Sure enough, Zach had broken his right leg.

Guess who drove home!

My friend, Beth, became engaged and upon hearing the news, I was thrilled for her and her fiancé, Phil. Two months before the wedding, an invitation was sent out by her mom for a surprise bridal shower.

Happily, I responded that I would be attending the shower, but unfortunately, it was also time for me to think about the choice of gift that could be bought and not duplicated by anyone else. Knowing that Beth had already received numerous engagement gifts, the reality of such a thing happening was plausible because she was not registered in any stores.

One night, a week before the party, I was still pondering in my mind what to buy for this bridal event. Finally, it became distinctly clear to me that my only option was to call Beth's mother to ask what items were missing from my friend's inventory of necessities. Since it was late in the evening, this task was put on my to-do list for the next morning and with a plan in mind, I fell into a fitful sleep.

I awoke in the morning laughing to myself because of a silly dream that I had experienced during the night. The dream consisted of me buying a toaster oven for Beth, costing $2,500. *Gee,* I thought, *for that kind of money, it should come with a chef.* Thinking no more about the absurdity of this fantasy, I dialed Beth's mother to ask the question that was obviously in the forefront of my mind.

After exchanging pleasantries regarding the family, the upcoming wedding and the weather, I inquired as to what gift could be purchased for Beth's upcoming shower. Her mother eagerly told me that her daughter was in need of a toaster oven. This request, of course, could not be fulfilled until I told her about my dream from the night before, which I did. We both laughed. Thanking her for her helpful input, I hung up the phone, still amused by the exorbitant-costing gift message that I received the night before in my dream—or should I say nightmare.

The next day, I put Beth's present high on my shopping list and took the short ride to a local department store to buy the toaster oven for the soon-to-be bride. I slid into the seat of the brand-new luxury car that Zach had recently purchased for me and carefully drove it to the back parking lot of the store. Logically, my hope was that it would be safer and less vulnerable to damage if parked there.

I made sure to situate my car in an area where there were at least three other automobiles nearby, but not too near to my magnificent vehicle. I got out of the car, locked the door and took one last look back to make sure my new wheels were safe. Like a woman with a mission, I walked through the back door of the store, headed straight for the housewares department, quickly picked out a toaster oven that I deemed to be suitable for Beth, paid for it (it wasn't $2,500) and left. The time period in which this shopping event took place was at most fifteen minutes.

With my new purchase in hand, I quickly walked back to my car, which was sitting alone, with the same autos surrounding it as when I had arrived in the lot earlier. But while approaching my vehicle, I noticed something different on the doors of the driver's side. Getting closer to it, the realization struck me that the entire area was totally scratched either by another car or by an object that must have been deliberately used to do the damage.

I stood there bemoaning the fate of what was once the most beautiful automobile in the world. My initial reaction to this personal misfortune was just to stand there and stare at it, unable to move. What was my next move? I decided to go home and telephone Zach in order to inform him of this latest crisis.

Of course, Zach was not very happy with the news from my phone call and after a few choice words, he told me to go to the local automobile body shop to get an estimate of what it would cost to fix. I went immediately to show John, the proprietor of the business, my badly damaged car.

John walked around the entire car, wrote some notes and turned to me with a grim face. "Well, I'm sorry to have to tell you that the damage repair will cost you $2,500."

Can you believe this story? It actually did cost me $2,500 to buy Beth a toaster oven.

Who says that dreams can't turn into reality!

Zach and I owned a speedboat that we used for recreational purposes. One Saturday morning, he and his friend Vinnie decided to go fishing for the day. Zach said he would be home in time for dinner. My intuition told me that he should not take out the boat because there was a problem with the engine.

I told him about the fear that I had, but he said that he knew about the engine's problem and consequently had it repaired just recently. But I was still feeling that a fire would happen and, as a result, I knew that it was important to fight him regarding the day's plan. He could not be convinced to change his mind.

Just as my intuition had predicted, the engine caught fire and Zach had to call the Coast Guard. He returned home early in the afternoon and told me that the engine that had been repaired was fine. The other engine (it was a dual-engine boat) was the one that caught fire.

The man just doesn't learn!

Here is another story about boats. This one was really quite an experience.

The forecast was for rain, and Zach and I had plans to take our boat, which was called Lucky Four, out into the ocean. As soon as I heard the weatherman's forecast, my psychic hearing began receiving a clear message, warning me to cancel the plans.

After considering what was being told to me, I really got nervous and then strongly relayed my feelings to Zach. It seemed logical to me that we should reschedule the outing for another day.

Then, suddenly, my already-received message was seconded by a vision of me attempting to dock the boat. This psychic picture was even more disconcerting considering because I had no formal education in boating. I feared and yet respected the water because I did not know how to swim. Even though there were life jackets onboard, an uncomfortable feeling always left me anxious regarding the safety of any boat outing. I don't know why I even agreed to go to begin with.

When I shared this psychic picture with Zach, as usual,

he told me not to worry. He said that he, as well as his friend Vinnie (see last story), who Zach had invited along with us, were very well equipped to handle any emergency. Vinnie's wife was also coming on the boat trip with us. She was just about as knowledgeable as I was on the subject, if not less so. Zach said that my boating expertise would not be needed during the trip and kept laughing while saying, "What are you worried about? You worry too much." When had I heard that before?

So, off we went into what seemed the middle of the ocean. The day started out overcast and eventually, a tremendous fog overtook the sky. When it started to rain, I realized that it was important for me to tell Zach that we needed to go back and return the boat to the marina. As I spoke, I turned to look at Zach and, to my dismay, saw that he and his friend Vinnie were seasick to the point that they couldn't even stand up. They were both vomiting and moaning but not more than I, who had to take control of the vessel.

It was now my responsibility to guide the boat back to safety. The boat didn't have a functioning compass, and the phones were also not operational, so this negated the possibility of the Coast Guard getting involved. The fog became so dense that I was unable to see anything in front of me. Whatever it is that watches over helpless boaters was definitely watching over all of us that day because, through some form of good fortune, I was able to steer the boat into the slip of the marina. The name Lucky Four was certainly apropos for this boating crew on that day.

Talk about *pier* pressure. Anonymous source, as usual,

you were right!

One morning, after waking up, a vision of Zach receiving a driving summons that day played out in mind. After telling him what the visual picture was indicating to me, I warned him that he had better wear his seat belt, obey the speed limit and not park where prohibited. Of course, he told me again that I worry too much.

Zach came marching into the house that evening fuming that my prediction came true again. He had answered his cell phone without a hands-free device and was quickly pulled over by a police officer.

I just love it when I prove that man wrong!

The date of February fourteenth, Valentine's Day, was fast approaching and Zach and I decided to celebrate this romantic holiday by going to a local restaurant for dinner. Since Zach was not planning to work on that day, he told me that he wanted to dine early, so that the usual Valentine's Day crowd would not hinder the wait for seating or the service that would be provided. I agreed and with this in mind, I made a reservation for 5:00 p.m.

When the actual day arrived, the little voice in my head kept telling me that I needed to change the reservation for two hours later, which would make it 7:00 p.m. I did not know why, but it just kept telling me to move the appointment two hours ahead.

When I approached Zach regarding my psychic feeling in reference to changing the time to 7:00 p.m., he fought me on it. He said, "Joy, you always like to eat early and since I'm off today, let's go at five, when the restaurant opens. Everything will be fine. We'll leave the house early and get home before it gets too late. We'll beat the crowd."

As usual, against my better judgment, I agreed, and I proceeded to get ready for the evening. Since it was a rainy night, it made sense to me to take an umbrella and a scarf, aside from taking my purse. But for some reason, I felt the need to take a first aid kit. It was always prudent to be prepared in case of an emergency, I thought.

We left the house and headed for the restaurant at 4:30 p.m. Due to the poor visibility, I was very cognizant of the fact that Zach drove very carefully to our destination. This cautionary measure pleased me.

As our vehicle approached the intersection of the street where the restaurant was located, a stop sign loomed a short distance ahead. Our car slowly came to rest alongside it while Zach waited to steer into a left turn. On the adjacent street, a speeding car, the driver of which was not respecting the fact that the street was wet and slippery, came charging towards us and sideswiped our car while making a turn. No one was injured but upon inspection of our automobile, we learned that significant damage had been sustained. Fortunately, the first-aid kit was not needed.

I immediately dialed 911 from my cell phone and waited with Zach for the local police department to come to the location of the accident. Due to the inclement weather that night, a patrol car did not arrive for another hour.

The written report of the accident, plus the exchanging of licenses, registrations and insurance cards, took an additional hour. Guess what time we walked into the restaurant. You guessed it! Seven o'clock.

I can't say that I wasn't warned, but you know who wouldn't listen to me!

Here is another psychic revelation that unfortunately happened to Zach and me.

It was a cold, winter Sunday and Zach asked me if I would agree to take a car ride out east to his favorite restaurant. As soon as he made the suggestion, the sound of a loud crash echoed in my ears. It sounded like metal hitting metal.

Upon receiving this psychic message about an accident, I was quick to nix the idea of a car ride that day because it was obvious to me that our vehicle would be involved in some type of incident. I could even visualize the car headlights being broken as well as glass on the ground. Zach promised me that he would take extra precautions to make it a safe drive and once again, like a fool, I agreed to go even though the ending of the day's events was right in front of my eyes.

So, off we went to our destination, with me hoping against hope that my vision was incorrect. The closer we got to the restaurant, the more my neck started to ache. For some reason, it began to feel stiff.

Suddenly, Zach made a sharp turn, lost control of the

steering wheel and crashed the car into the metal guardrail. It was unavoidable because there was no shoulder on the road. My neck snapped back and I instantly felt whiplash in that area. Zach was stunned and needed to calm down regarding this turn of events. As predicted that morning, the glass headlights broke and the remnants lay on the road as well as on the guardrail.

Needless to say, we never completed our trip to the restaurant, which I knew would happen from my vision that very morning. I had been a witness to this incident and didn't listen to my own message.

Anonymous source, I'm sorry that I didn't listen to you. This was an accident waiting to happen!

Chapter Three

Scary Times

Most of us who were already born at the time when John F. Kennedy was assassinated remember where we were when we heard the shocking news bulletin regarding his death.

On the night before Friday, November 22, 1963, the nightly news stated that President Kennedy was going to be in Dallas the next day. When I heard the newscaster's report of that story, my thoughts went into psychic mode. My mind kept saying that the president should have the convertible top up on the limousine and he should keep moving because there will be danger. I then saw in my mind shovels of dirt being thrown on top of him. The scene was taking place in a cemetery.

If he kept moving, he would be fine, but I felt that he was too trusting and was definitely in jeopardy. This picture was hard to believe but seemed so real.

Nevertheless, I was in the same state of disbelief as everyone else when I learned that our beloved president had been assassinated. If only I could have relived the day before it happened and warned him.

But who would have listened to a fifteen-year-old girl?

At the age of sixteen, I belonged to a sorority in high school with the honor of being the youngest member in it. My boyfriend, Ray, was a senior and since I was employed in a real job earning real money afterschool, all the girls thought of me as quite grown up and mature.

One day, a group of my sorority sisters decided to take a trip to a large amusement park in New Jersey. Eager to go for the excitement of being there but not really caring to go on any of the rides, I didn't express any real desire to participate in the main reason for being there—which was, again, going on the rides. It seemed to me that many of those so-called entertainment delights seemed risky, if not downright dangerous.

When we arrived at the park, we all stood there for a few minutes, watching the faces of the seemingly brave young adults scurrying around, looking for their next adventures to go on. Suddenly, a vision came into my mind. I saw a teenage boy falling from one particular ride. After seeing this and then telling my friends what I sensed, my prophesy was concluded with the words "there will be a problem here." My feeling was that a specific ride was either defective or lacking the proper equipment to protect its riders. My friends all stood there staring at me.

Of course, no one wanted to listen to me, and they were now all viewing me as being immature and a killjoy. Trying to get my reputation back, I decided to chance the day's activities by allowing my psychic message to take a backseat to my social life.

Unfortunately for me, all the girls wanted to go on the ride that I felt was the troublesome one. What were my choices? As much as I believed in my premonition, it wouldn't have been appreciated by anyone if the day at the amusement park was ruined by me, the newest and youngest girl in the sorority. My friends would not invite me to go anywhere or do anything with them again.

So, while following my friends onto the platform of the ride with a strong feeling of apprehension, I meekly asked the attendant who was in charge what was involved regarding the dynamics of this particular ride. After his explanation to me of the details concerning what to anticipate, I climbed down from the ride's landing area, leaving my friends behind. It was a little too daring for my liking. At that point, I didn't care what they thought about me. I stood off to the side, waiting for the ride to start. The image of a young man falling and dying became stronger and stronger.

Within two minutes of the ride's beginning, one of the riders, a teenage boy, began to dangle from and then totally let go of a bar onto which he had been holding. He then hit the ground and lay there motionless. The ride came to a halt as all the participants, as well as the spectators, screamed in horror. Surprisingly, there was no type of safety net to shield all those involved who needed to be protected. The ride required that everyone had to fend for himself by holding on with two hands. Obviously, this teenager didn't do as instructed, which meant that he had been doomed from the onset. To me, it was amazing that no one had been hurt or killed up until that day.

My friends got off the ride and were so emotionally and physically shaken that they couldn't wait to leave the amusement park. Well, they couldn't say I didn't warn them.

I was no longer the immature one... I was the smart one!

One Saturday morning, I woke up with the words *thunder* and *bolt* ringing in my ears. Not sure if it was one word or two, I did know it was the warning of a negative happening. A traumatizing experience was on my radar and a fearful sensation was giving a warning of a happening in my near future.

It was a message that was difficult to figure out, but I knew that as the day's activities progressed, circumstances would eventually show the meaning.

My plans for the day included getting ready for a date with a really nice young man named Paul, who I had been dating for a few weeks. He was nineteen, drove a car and seemed to be the type of guy every girl looks for at that age — or any age. I was very impressed with his easygoing disposition and looked forward to seeing him that evening.

Of course, being only seventeen years of age gave me the luxury of not thinking about any type of commitment. I hadn't even graduated from high school, and my life was open to many decisions yet to be made.

Paul came for me at 7:00 p.m., as promised, and we left my house to go to a local restaurant. We had a leisurely dinner and talked nonstop until we finished our coffee and dessert.

As we were about to leave the restaurant, he asked me if I would come to see where he lived, which was in a trailer park. He had recently moved out of his parents' house and was very proud of his new living arrangements. Since it was early, I agreed to go see his mobile home, even though the weather had become unpleasant because it had started to rain.

Paul drove us there while telling me about the way it was going to be furnished and the eventual plans he had to get married and start a family.

When I walked in the door of the trailer, I became very apprehensive because the living area was very small. Never being able to acclimate myself to staying in any confined spaces and always thinking of myself as claustrophobic, these were not comfortable surroundings for me. I almost felt as if there were a tent over me. The whole scene made me anxious to leave, even if it meant going into the rainy night.

While I reached to open the front door, Paul yelled to me, "Wait!" I turned around and saw that he was holding in his hand an open box with a diamond engagement ring inside. There I stood, literally shocked. We had never discussed any type of marital agreement or arrangement with one another. Thanking Paul for the proposal, I explained that my young age hindered me from even thinking about marriage.

The evening's turn of events surprised both of us. I had not expected to be proposed to, and he had not expected to be turned down. This was an awkward situation, and my anxiety to leave was definitely growing stronger.

Now the rain was pounding incessantly on the roof. There was nonstop thunder in my ears and brilliant lightning in the summer sky, which was shining through the small windows of the room in which we stood. Paul told me that he would get an umbrella and we would leave.

I waited patiently by the door as he went to look for one. But instead of bringing out the promised rain protector from the closet, he brought out a hammer and nails. He walked quickly past me and over to the only exit in the room. Paul told me that I was going to be held hostage there until my answer to his proposal was "yes." He bolted the door closed with the nails and we stood looking at each other. There was my answer to *thunder* and *bolt*.

Feeling terrified, I quickly told him that my mind had suddenly changed and his marriage proposal would be accepted. He happily took the nails out of the door. I ran past him and out the door as fast as my feet would carry me. I felt my heart beating at a tempo of unparalleled force because of my frantic urgency to get away from Paul. For some strange reason, he did not follow me. He must have realized what a fool he had made of himself by locking me in the trailer.

Why would anyone want to marry someone who didn't feel the same way?

Zach and I purchased tickets for a concert at Carnegie Hall. Two of my favorite performers were scheduled to appear and since I had never seen them live on stage, this was an evening about which I was quite excited.

We arrived early, found our seats and waited patiently for the show to start. As the performance began, I received a message from my inner voice. The communication was a whisper, telling me to leave the theatre quickly due to a fire. I turned to Zach and said, "There is going to be a fire here. We need to get out fast. Get up and run."

He in turn said, "Do you smell or see smoke?"

I said, "No."

He answered, "Just stay in your seat and watch the show. Enjoy yourself!"

Since our seats were in the balcony, I knew that the smart thing to do was to leave right then. I was afraid of being trampled. Since Zach didn't believe me, I got up and left. Excusing myself for disturbing the other concertgoers in my row, I moved calmly and quickly while making my way downstairs, and I eventually found the exit door of the theater.

While standing outside by myself for several minutes, doubts regarding my feelings started to emerge. Everyone was inside, enjoying the performance, and there I was, standing alone, waiting for a fire to happen. Could I have been incorrect? Was this a misjudgment? It seemed so weird, but the feeling that it was going to happen was still within me.

Suddenly, all the building doors opened and the theatre began to empty. Zach was soon standing at my side, explaining that the audience was sent outside because there was an ongoing blaze happening due to faulty electrical wires.

When the audience returned to the theater after the fire engines left, we all received ticket refunds. It was quite an experience for all of us.

Tell me, Zach, did you enjoy the show?

While we are on the subject of fire, here is another story that might intrigue you.

One Saturday afternoon, Zach wanted to have lunch in a well-known and highly rated restaurant. It didn't take much reasoning on Zach's part to convince me to go, and soon we were headed in that direction. It was going to be a lovely afternoon for both of us.

As we approached our destination, my mind's eye showed me a picture of flames. *This is not going to be such good idea after all,* I thought, and of course I conveyed my feelings to Zach.

Unfortunately, Zach was not going to be persuaded out of going to this particular café. His mind was made up and his appetite was ready. As usual, this was going to be a problem because he told me that I was worrying for nothing and that he was not changing his mind.

Realizing that the restaurant was busy because it was lunch hour, I made a specific request for a table near the door. Unfortunately, the only table available was in the back corner, which would have given us privacy. Under normal circumstances, I would have been thrilled to be seated there, but considering my earlier psychic vision, this was not an area in which I would feel comfortable. After telling the hostess that we would wait for a table near the door, Zach and I argued about my recent prophesy while standing in the lobby.

Finally, a table close to the entrance became available for us. We sat down, ordered and began to eat as soon as the food arrived. I stayed calm only because the doorway was within my sight and therefore an easy, quick exit could be made. Even though Zach complained every time the door opened and let in a draft, as well as about the lack of privacy and poor service due to the fact that the table wasn't near the kitchen, I reminded him of my prediction.

After we finished eating, I was anxious to leave but Zach wanted dessert. I became increasingly stressed regarding the length of time that we were spending in the restaurant. The waitress was nowhere to be found, and finally Zach said that when she came into view, we would get the check, pay it and leave.

Moments later, the restaurant owner appeared, stood in front of the customers and made an announcement, requesting that everyone exit the premises because there was an out-of-control kitchen fire. The man was so calm that, quite honestly, I was very impressed. It was obvious to me that he didn't want his clientele to panic.

There could have been a chaotic situation if he hadn't set the tone of the moment with the announcement. He told us all not to worry about paying for the food we had ordered and even told his patrons to take their food with them as they left. Many of the customers who were still eating did just that.

Since Zach and I were near the door, we were the first ones out of the eatery. Fortunately, the restaurant emptied quickly, with all those involved staying calm.

The parking lot was a sea of people running to their vehicles. As soon as our car reached the street, I saw the entire restaurant explode into flames, just as my vision had shown me an hour prior.

Unfortunately, I found the free lunch that everyone looks for!

This next story is one that was too close to reality for my liking. If this story didn't prove that premonitions and destiny are real, nothing would.

One day, Zach and I, along with our friends Karen and Jeff, decided to book a trip on a cruise ship that was leaving from a port in Florida. The itinerary required that we take an airplane from New York in order to board the ship. I was busy shopping and planning for weeks in preparation for this vacation and was greatly looking forward to it.

I was not aware of any problems with the plane when I boarded it and was eagerly anticipating a nice flight. However, as the plane taxied down the runway, a feeling of anxiety encompassed me. Ignoring what the take-off rules dictated, I quickly stood up, took out my tarot cards from the overhead compartment and decided to confirm my suspicions, because normally I am not afraid to fly.

Just as I suspected, the cards indicated that there was something menacingly wrong with the plane. (All of this happened in a matter of minutes, but it seemed like it took hours.) After shuffling the cards and receiving the same answers each time, the realization of an impending incident was becoming quite obvious to me. Not knowing what to do regarding this possibly catastrophic event, I leaned over to Zach, who was watching me, and said, "This plane is going to crash."

He said, "Keep your voice down and don't embarrass me." My friends, who were sitting in front of us, echoed what my husband said. They were all laughing at me. At that moment, I knew that the matter was going to have to be taken care of by me and me alone.

I got up from my seat and headed for a flight attendant. I was hyperventilating and clutching my chest, feigning a heart attack in progress. Knowing that I had to be dramatic in order to be taken seriously, I Immediately told the flight attendant about my conjured condition. She told me that she would inform the pilot.

As she was headed towards the cockpit, the pilot's voice was heard over the intercom: "Ladies and gentlemen, I'm sorry but I'm going to have to turn this plane around and return to the terminal because there is an electrical problem. We will be delayed approximately one hour."

Needless to say, I was very relieved, and, happily, the plane never left with anyone onboard. An hour later, the pilot informed us that the problem was much greater than he had anticipated. I had to do some fast talking to the flight attendant, telling her that I was feeling better and that an ambulance wasn't needed.

All the passengers were placed on another plane that took us to our destination without any problems.

Still embarrassed?

On one weekend afternoon, I couldn't shake the feeling that my life was in danger. There was something terribly wrong, and once again that little voice warned me that I had better pay attention to my surroundings.

I needed to do the food shopping for the following week, which was a normal routine for me and quite honestly, my premonition was that it was safer to be out of the house than in it. I told Zach about my fear over and over, but once again he laughed at me, saying that my feelings were overly dramatic.

I insisted that he stay home while I went out shopping so that my return would not be to an empty house, and he dutifully promised to do just that, even though he thought I was being silly. For some strange reason, I didn't feel any danger for him; it was only for me.

I left the house to go to the supermarket at noon and returned an hour later. When I drove my car into the driveway, the fact that Zach's car was no longer parked in its usual spot left me in fear. I was truly frightened to go into the house if no one was home.

Unfortunately, not foreseeing that Zach wasn't going to be home as promised, I had purchased food that needed to be refrigerated, so there was no time to dwell on my doubts or hesitations. While getting out of the car, I panned the immediate area surrounding the house. Seeing no one and nothing suspicious, I brought the bundles into the house while still not letting down my guard. The dread had not lessened even though everything looked fine.

The house was completely quiet and I started putting the groceries away. While busily arranging the items on the shelves, I suddenly felt my hair being pulled. At the same time my face was repeatedly pushed into the cabinets. The assault seemed endless, and something that could not be stopped. The intruder attacked me viciously, hitting me with an iron pipe. The pain was unbearable. Luckily for me, a neighbor heard my screams and came running into the house. I yelled, "Call 911!"

The assailant ran out the door, leaving me lying on the floor in a pool of blood. The ambulance came quickly and took me to the hospital, where I was diagnosed with multiple injuries. Once again, that little voice in my head had been correct.

Zach came to the emergency room a short time after I was admitted and walked past me, not recognizing me due to my injuries. He again said that he could not believe that my premonition was accurate.

The intruder was caught and jailed, but two months later we moved out of that house and to this day, I can honestly say that attack was the most terrifying experience of my life. The nightmares haven't stopped and probably never will.

Never assume that you are safe in your own home!

It was the Fourth of July, a hot sticky Thursday. Zach and I had been invited to my friend Gina's house for a barbecue and pool party. It was billed as a fun-filled day. All of her friends and neighbors were invited and everyone except for me was looking forward to having a good time.

I didn't want to go because from the time I received the invitation, I knew a child was going to drown that day. Hesitating to say anything because there were many, including Gina, who would dismiss this type of warning, I just had to pray for inclement weather.

Unfortunately, there was no rain in the forecast, so the party proceeded as planned. One by one, the cars pulled up to the house, bringing the partygoers who gleefully ran towards the house with floats and pool toys. The party began.

As the day progressed, everyone appeared to be having an enjoyable time. Tim, Gina's husband, was busy at the grill and all of Gina's friends and their children were in the pool or on the pool deck, developing or increasing their much-desired suntans.

After the food was eaten and the sun had set, all the attendees who were still present at the party went into the house for dessert and coffee. Thankfully, the children came inside, too. In addition to the end-of-meal refreshments, music and dancing were on the agenda.

I was very relieved that the day had gone smoothly, with no incidents. Of course, it meant that my premonition had not come to pass, which was certainly a relief. If I had to describe what kind of day it was for me, it could be said that my role in the party's activities was that of an observer and not a participant. This was not surprising but rather expected, considering my fear from the time of the receipt of the invitation.

Even though it was evening, I kept glancing at the pool through the glass sliding doors to make sure that no children strayed outside unattended. I even locked the door myself to make sure that the toddlers were unable to leave. But relaxation was still not on my program because the negativity I sensed was becoming overwhelming.

The messages that I received kept showing that the children needed to be sheltered. It was such an uncomfortable predicament because I was the only one aware of the tragic eventuality that I was foreseeing. This meant that the responsibility was borne by me alone. The festive party continued, with no one aware of my psychic prediction.

Suddenly, the mood of the moment was interrupted by loud screams coming from the rear yard. As all the guests listened to the terrifying cries, everyone's attention became focused on the pool, where a man not many of us knew jumped into the water. He was trying to rescue a little boy whom we hadn't even seen before that moment.

I later found out that the little boy was Gina's neighbor's nephew. He had wandered in probably looking for his mother, who was present at the party. His father had put him to bed and, thinking that his son was asleep, came to join his wife for the end of the evening. As he approached Gina's house, his son, who had obviously left his bed, was following and must have jumped or fallen into the pool.

The father, seeing his son in the water, jumped in to save him. My vision of that fateful drowning had come to pass. All of my watching and anticipating couldn't prevent the tragic eventuality of that day.

You can't fight destiny!

I had an eye doctor appointment one afternoon at five o'clock. This was the only appointment that was available that week and since I was long overdue for a checkup, there was no choice for me but to take it.

When the date came, I spent the entire day in stressful torment about whether or not to keep the appointment. A weird feeling kept gnawing at me to reschedule. Why was this allotted time giving me such severe uncertainty? After all, it was merely a visit to the eye doctor. It was difficult for me to make any sense of it.

When I called the doctor's office to confirm the appointment, I was told that he was going to be there as scheduled, so that meant that this part of the anticipated problem was fine. I was once again back to the search for a clue to or reasonable explanation for my feeling of such intense anxiety.

The hour arrived for me to leave the house, and I drove to my destination still wondering what was causing my uneasiness. Many thoughts rushed through my mind, the leading one being the possibility of a car accident. It was rush hour and the traffic was building, which made this the most plausible and logical answer.

But, eventually—and happily—I pulled into the parking lot, thinking, *So far, so good.*

Upon entering the lobby, I looked around carefully, still questioning my feelings of trepidation. After pressing the elevator button, I waited patiently for my ride to arrive. Up until then, there had been no visible explanations regarding the nervous and stressful apprehension I was experiencing. Maybe this time my intuition was just wrong.

My desire was just to get this doctor appointment over with once and for all. At that point, I made up my mind that too much negative energy had gone into the appointment, and I was not going to let it ruin the rest of the day.

When the elevator doors finally opened, no one walked out. After I entered the elevator car, the doors closed tightly and I was glad for it. Being the only one in the car relieved me of the fear of being attacked by a stranger. Besides, the ride, for me, was only up one floor

Unfortunately, my thoughts were starting to drift again. They were playing all different kinds of possible morbid scenarios regarding the various events of the day, leading up to the situation I was experiencing at that moment. The sinking feeling that had been pervasive in my mind throughout the last several hours was still dominating my reality.

As the car ascended, I heard a noise that sounded like a thud and suddenly, the elevator stopped. An oppressive fear came over me. While yelling out to no one in particular about my predicament, I pressed the elevator buttons, but it was to no avail. The elevator was stuck in between the lobby and the first floor.

Wild thoughts, the result of panic, went through my mind. Now I was sorry that no one was on the elevator with me. Aside from the fact that I was claustrophobic (remember the mobile home story?), who would want to be alone in a situation like that?

My heart started to race and I began to get gloomy ideas, such as the possibility that due to the lateness of the hour, no one would know that I was even in there. My reasoning continued that all the occupants of the building would leave the building via the steps after realizing that the elevator was broken. There was even the possibility of my being left there overnight.

Meanwhile, I just kept yelling as loudly as possible while pressing the emergency button. Hearing no response from outside, I became more and more distraught regarding my dilemma. Drenched in sweat, with my heart pounding and my mind thinking, I realized that I had found the reason for my disturbing gut feeling that day—big time.

Finally, after twenty minutes of crying and jabbing buttons, I heard the clanking of tools in the elevator shaft and then, at last, my little dungeon slowly continued its ride upwards. Suddenly, I heard a man's voice yelling to me, "Help is here. Everything is going to be okay. Just hang in there." The elevator came to a halt and within seconds, the doors were pried open. My hero that day was a repairman, a master mechanic sent from a place of wondrous miracles.

I said to him, "I love you. You are my idol." He laughed, took my hand and guided me out of the elevator.

While patting my wrist, he said to me, "I'm sorry for your ordeal."

I proceeded to the eye doctor's suite of offices and walked in, shaking, sweating and with makeup running down my face. The doctor, who was standing by the reception desk, didn't even notice my condition, which must have been obvious only to me. He said, "You're late. What happened?"

"What happened? I've been stuck in the elevator for twenty minutes."

He answered me by calmly saying, "We always have trouble with that elevator."

I had gone to this doctor for many, many years and never had a problem with the elevator till that day. Needless to say, I walked down the steps when leaving, vowing never to use that elevator again.

When I returned home and told Zach the story, he said, "This could only happen to you."

Another lesson for me to listen to myself regarding psychic messages!

One day, Zach telephoned from his job and asked me to make a bank deposit for him. He told me where he had put the money that was to be deposited. After hanging up the phone, I immediately sought out the location of the cash, counted the money and then filled out a deposit slip, attaching the money to it.

I drove my car to the crowded bank parking lot and went inside the massive building in which the bank was housed.

There were unusually long lines of customers. Knowing that there was nothing that could be done about it, I waited along with everyone else as the rows of patrons moved slowly forward.

Suddenly, I heard a familiar voice whispering in my psychic hearing: "Something is not right with Grant." Thinking that I didn't know anyone by the name of Grant, I dismissed the message.

Soon, the line I was waiting in began moving ahead more quickly and shortly after, I reached the window where the bank teller was waiting to serve me. I handed the young woman the deposit slip along with the cash and waited for her to process the transaction.

She took it from me and counted the money carefully. After giving me a quick glance, she left her post and went into the back room of the bank. I stood there patiently, thinking that there was a problem with the computers, which often happened. Again, I heard the little voice emphatically saying, "Something wrong with Grant!" But the message still meant nothing to me.

I stood there and waited, but I also noticed that the bank customers in the other lines were being taken care of by their individual tellers and were then leaving. The five-minute wait had now turned into twenty minutes. I couldn't understand where the teller for my line had gone. She was no where in sight.

Without warning, the door of the bank opened and several policemen, along with one man whom I later found out was a Secret Service agent, filed through. They quickly came inside the room, which was at that time still filled with customers. The group sprinted over to me with a seemingly definitive mission in mind. All the bank customers stood in their respective lines, staring at me. Instead of thinking that I had done anything wrong, my thoughts were that the bank was being held up.

The police officer who appeared to be in charge started the conversation, telling me that I had to accompany these gentlemen to the police precinct. Totally confused, I explained to all of them that I had not witnessed any robbery. One of the policemen told me that I was the one who committed a crime. It was then relayed to me that one of the fifty-dollar bills—bearing President Grant's picture—in my deposit was counterfeit.

All of these men escorted me to an empty corner of the bank and began questioning me about where I had gotten the money. I explained that Zach had cashed his paycheck at another bank and that this fifty-dollar bill had been part of the transaction.

I took my cell phone out of my purse, dialed Zach's work phone number and was told by the woman who answered that he wasn't in the office. I tried his cell phone but, unfortunately, it was not turned on. Then, one of the agents asked me how long I had been circulating counterfeit money. I explained that I had no knowledge of any of the bills being bogus. They all continued to question me and finally decided that it was an honest mistake, which it was.

Since that experience, I let Zach do all the banking. But now I know—and so do you—that President Grant's picture is on the fifty-dollar bill!

My friend Sheila was between marriages and was looking to meet a man to make her life more meaningful. One day, she asked me to come to her home to do a tarot card reading. As always, I was happy to oblige her because she was, as many of my other friends were, very supportive of my career, and I wanted to try to give something back to each of them.

As she shuffled the cards, she kept telling me about her desire to find a man with whom she could share the rest of her life. This was a major issue for her.

When I put the cards on the table, I noticed that they were reflecting nothing of her desires for domestic happiness and emotional fulfillment. The tarot cards were talking about her mother, saying that she was going to have a shortened life span. I quickly told Sheila to be quiet about her future husband.

"The cards are talking about your mom," I told her. "They are saying that she only has three months to live." I could not believe that my cards were telling one of my dearest friends such bad news.

"There is nothing wrong with my mother's health," Sheila replied, her eyes widening. "My father is the sickly one. You must be mistaken."

But I definitely saw that it was her mother. Sheila had a very close and loving relationship with her mom and therefore refused to believe my reading. I didn't want to belabor the subject because it was upsetting to both of us. I put my tarot cards away and did no more readings that day.

Unfortunately, but predictably, my cards were right again. Three months later, Sheila's mother died of a heart attack.

Sheila called me in disbelief. "How did you know?" she asked.

I simply told her, "It was in the cards."

It's no wonder that my friends are afraid to come near me, but I don't cause these happenings. I am just the messenger!

Wait until you hear this story. It taught us why responsibilities for other people's children can be *so* stressful!

Tina and Marty needed their children taken care of on the day they were moving into their new house. Since Zach and I were their best friends, they asked us if we could do that for them. Now, the question for us was, what should we do with a two-year-old and a six-year-old?

After much thinking and discussion, we decided that an amusement park would be a good source of entertainment for all of us. We plotted the day's events in advance and ended up with what we thought was a well-organized plan to entertain our little charges.

When the day arrived, Zach and I went to Tina and Marty's house, gathered up the children and their toys, and moved them quickly to our car. We left their stressed parents, who were carefully guiding the moving men as to the order of the boxes that should be carried out to the van. It gave us a good feeling to be helping out our friends.

The day started with breakfast, which we had in a diner near the amusement park. After that, we were ready to make the big plunge into what we were hoping would be a day to remember.

As we went through the gate of the park, I noticed at once how large the crowd was. Seeing the masses of people there made me even more attuned to the importance of proper oversight of both of the boys. I carried Jeffrey, the two-year-old, and assumed (never assume) that Zach would take care of Steven.

Unfortunately, Zach and I became separated at one point because of the throng of people. Add to that the fact that there were many distractions, including rides and refreshments. With all that going on, I didn't notice that Steven had disappeared from view.

When I eventually realized he was absent, I thought perhaps he had gone to the restroom. In actuality, I was hoping that this was the case, because I had no idea where he was.

"Zach, where is Steven?" I asked tentatively. Zach, who was busy watching the rides we were passing, looked at me quizzically.

"I thought that he was walking with you," he answered. "Steven told me that he wanted to walk with Jeffrey and you."

Any parent who has ever noticed his or her child missing in a similar circumstance, whether it's at an amusement park or a store or in any type of a crowded situation, knows what a sickening feeling it is. It is almost indescribable. You can imagine what the feeling is when it isn't even your own child who is missing, though the responsibility is yours.

Not knowing what to do, but in an absolute panic, I ran, still holding Jeffrey, to a security guard who was standing not far from us. I asked him if Steven could be paged. Not even waiting for an answer, I noticed a police officer nearby, so I thankfully ran to him for help. A feeling of total hysteria was starting to overtake me. The police officer tried to calm me down, but the only thing that would relax me would be finding my friend's son.

Suddenly, I decided that my psychic skills would be the only way for me to solve this problem. Knowing that it was necessary to make my mind still in order to get a sense of Steven's location, I closed my eyes and tried to compose myself even though my heart was racing furiously.

I inhaled slowly, and suddenly, I smelled the stench of an animal zoo. I asked the police officer if there were an area in the park devoted to animals. The police officer told me that there was indeed a small petting zoo on the other side of the park, which was a distance from where we were standing.

We all ran quickly, following the policeman, and finally Steven was spotted. There he stood, feeding some bread to the ducks, completely unaware of the drama that his absence had caused. I cried, realizing how this situation could have ended.

Anonymous source…that was a close one!

Chapter Four

Volunteering, Jobs and Careers

I became a hospital volunteer while in my teens. I enjoyed interacting with the patients who were confined to their rooms. Many of the elderly had no immediate family visiting them on a regular basis, so I tried to cheer them up by telling them funny stories. The ailments varied from minor ailments to incurable cancer.

Not being able to help those with the latter problem, I would sit next to them and hold their hands. Sometimes we would laugh together and sometimes we would cry together.

One afternoon, I was sitting with a patient named Edna. She was in the last days of her illness. We sat talking with each other. Suddenly, I saw a halo over Edna's head. She looked like an angel with a special sparkle surrounding her. My next feeling was that of being pricked like a pin cushion. This sensation indicated to me that her time had come to proceed to wherever souls go when they leave this world.

Hearing my psychic voice telling me to exit the room because Edna wanted to spare me the experience of seeing her actually die, I told Edna that there was something that needed my attention in the next room.

After explaining to her that I would be back shortly, I left the room, knowing that when I returned to her bedside I would find this lovely woman's life force gone. On my way out the door, I said to her, "I love you, Edna." It was important to me that these words be the last ones she heard before departing this life.

After coming back into the room moments later, the message sent to me from my anonymous source was verified: she had indeed passed on. I was so glad that I had taken the time to say goodbye and hopefully made her passing a little more comfortable. I write this through a veil of tears because even now, many years later, I remember her as a wise and remarkable woman.

The time that we spend here is never wasted if we can give others positive recollections and loving memories of us!

Most of the evenings at the hospital where I volunteered were the same in the sense that they were joyful, with new life being born, or depressing, with the deaths of people of all ages.

I was standing in the emergency room when Lindsay was wheeled in on a stretcher. At first glance, she looked like many other teenage girls. She was wearing designer clothes, had braces on her teeth and was using cosmetics unsparingly to camouflage the acne on her otherwise pretty face. Her red hair was pulled back into a ponytail, which was held by a wide, white ribbon.

Upon studying her, I was able to witness what would be a tragedy for both her and her family. Focusing my mind on the situation showed me the permanent dilation of a blood vessel. I overheard Lindsay's mother telling the doctor who was assigned to the case that her daughter had fainted from a migraine headache. But my psychic vision was telling me that she had a brain aneurism and was in a coma.

Shortly after admission, Lindsay was rushed into an intensive care unit. Her hair was shaved off and wires were attached to the top of her head. I followed the entire scenario during the three days that she stayed in the hospital. She never regained consciousness and soon passed away in front of her distraught mother and father.

I did not know this teenager, but as a contemporary at the time, I could feel the pain of everyone concerned!

This is a story of an event that took place in 1964, when I worked at the New York World's Fair. It was an enjoyable job because it encouraged me to think of myself as very grown up.

Having access to all the pavilions, I would walk from one to another and tell any of the visitors who would listen about my employment there. It was much fun because the atmosphere seemed to resemble that of a vacation. The whole experience just made me feel quite important.

While employed in one of the restaurants, I met a very nice young girl by the name of Cathy. We worked together, Cathy as a waitress and me as the cashier. Since I knew only Cathy and not her family, it was a very strange phenomenon to me that one day, while I was standing near her, a vision came to me signifying that there would be a personal loss coming to this hardworking young woman. More specifically, I sensed it would involve an older woman, and that it would be her mother.

Not knowing how to tell Cathy this news, I blurted out to my new friend that she should spend more time with her mother because her mom had a declining health problem. I knew that her mother was going to die within six months, but even while realizing this, I rationalized that I didn't know Cathy well enough to be so blunt in my prediction.

Cathy, who was a very busy divorced young mother, was curious about why I would suggest that. She told me that her mother's health was fine. Cathy also explained that balancing caring for a baby with the demands of a work schedule required much time and energy. It was therefore difficult to have many visits with her mother. She expressed the hope of seeing her mom more often in the future, but her allotted free time was just too full and hectic right then.

Finally, I told Cathy that by the time she would be able to fit her mother into her schedule, it would be too late. Feeling strongly about this, I wouldn't dismiss the subject of her visiting her mom. Continuing to prod her, into more Mom time and inquiring whether Cathy was persuading her mother to visit the doctor, was something that had become a major issue in my mind.

Cathy wasn't totally convinced that I knew what I was talking about, but she later told me that she tried to convince her mother to go to the doctor for a checkup. However, whenever the subject came up between the two of them, her mother would say that she didn't think it was necessary to visit the doctor because she was feeling fine.

Five months went by and one day, Cathy didn't come in to work. When I inquired about her absence, I was informed that she was at her mother's funeral.

When Cathy came back to resume her job after the bereavement period was over, she informed me that her mother had died suddenly from a stroke. It had given no warning. But, thanks to my psychic intuition, she had been prepared for her mom's demise. Due to my advice, it seems, she had made the time to spend the last few months with her mother and was now grateful for it.

Now that I am older, the realization of the possible consequences that could have befallen me due to the fact that my dire prediction could have been misconstrued is something that I think about often. Cathy could have gotten very angry and therefore caused quite a problem for me. Fortunately, she believed that I had only good intentions, and she was not at all vindictive toward me.

We never knew how much time we have here on earth!

After my job at the New York World's Fair came to an end, I found employment in a department store. This was the type of job about which every girl my age dreamed. I was hired to be a flyer, which meant that I could be a substitute in any department that was missing personnel on a given day. It was interesting because each day was different. Also, it taught me how a substitute teacher feels.

When my friend Brenda got word that I was working in this particular store, she asked me if I could get her a job. After telling her that I would speak with someone in the personnel department, I fulfilled my promise and happily, the director hired her. So then, Brenda and I were both employed by the same store. She was placed in the refund department and seemed very content there.

In my position as a flyer, I would see Brenda each time a substitute was needed for someone who was missing in her area of the store. She appeared to be working diligently with the customers who were returning merchandise.

One time, while I was assigned to be on the second floor, which was where the refund department was situated, I decided that I would do a mental reading of Brenda. In my mind's eye, there she was, stealing money. It was an embarrassment for me, and I did not know how to handle the situation.

Finally, I asked her about what my vision had shown me. "Are you taking money that doesn't belong to you?" Of course, she denied it. I wasn't taking her word for it, though, because to me, it was already a fact.

I then told her that she was a liar and a thief, and she was therefore in an immense amount of trouble because she had been seen in the act of stealing. Brenda, believing that I had visually witnessed her taking the cash, confessed to it. She admitted to me that she was taking money on a regular basis.

I admonished her, saying that she was doing a terrible thing and that she was to stop immediately or I would report her. Brenda said that she would cease this behavior and actually did stop taking the store's money because she was afraid of being fired and arrested.

Just as I had known that she was stealing, I knew that she had stopped the activity. My mind's eye kept a check on her and periodically, my psychic vision would do a reading on her.

It's so sad when you do a friend a favor and then find that she can't be trusted!

It started out as an ordinary day. I returned home from school, ate dinner and, following my usual routine, began to get ready to go to my part-time job at the department store. Before leaving my house, for some unknown reason, I walked to a kitchen drawer, took out a flashlight and put it in my handbag. Thinking about it afterwards, I realized that while being aware of my action, I didn't know for what reason I did it. It was almost a subconscious move because a flashlight wasn't something that I would ordinarily need.

While driving to work, I noticed that several traffic lights weren't working. The thought of a power line problem in the area entered my mind, but soon left it. I really couldn't give it much attention because my means of transportation was actually my boyfriend's car, and it was important to give complete concentration to my driving. This was also the reason why I wasn't playing the car radio.

Upon arriving at my destination, I entered the employees' entrance located at the back of the store. It was late afternoon and the stairway leading to the employees' lounge was dark. I remembered the flashlight in my purse and quickly took it out, thinking that it was ideal that I had it on my person even though it was undecided in my mind as to why I had brought it with me.

My routine of punching in with my time card was disrupted when I discovered that the machine was out of order. It was then that my supervisor approached me and explained that all of New York and Long Island were in the midst of a major blackout. He let me sign in so that I could get paid for coming to work and then told me that it was alright for me to leave to go home. After he warned me to drive carefully, which was the understatement of the year, I left the store not knowing what circumstances were waiting for me out in the street.

The trip home was really scary. I was cognizant of the fact that there was no electricity for anyone. My hands clung to the steering wheel; I was fearful for my life and for my boyfriend's car. The street intersections were like battle zones, filled with vehicles trying to get through.

Finally, I returned to the street where I lived and drove carefully into the driveway while looking at all the houses on the block cloaked in darkness. After walking into my house, I discovered that my mother, whose only source of light was a candle, was frantically looking for the flashlight I had taken from the kitchen drawer earlier. After removing it from my handbag and handing it to her, I explained that I had taken it to work. When she asked me why I would take a flashlight to work, I simply answered, "That's a good question. I have no idea why. It just seemed that it was something that was necessary to be done."

I guess we all needed to go to the light that night…only we came back!

While working for the same department store, I was asked to model in a fashion show. Having never modeled before, it was both flattering and terrifying for me to walk down an actual runway.

The night of the event, I was waiting for my turn to get into position for my big debut when suddenly, a frightening feeling came over me. There was going to be a problem. The story of Henny Penny—"the sky is falling!"—came into my mind. I had no idea why a child's story would be invading my thoughts at a time like that.

Vacillating on whether or not to dwell on this message, I suddenly realized that it was my turn to show the many attendees of the evening's event the beautiful dress that had been chosen for me to wear. As I initiated my walk down the ramp, the feeling of the children's story became so intense that I decided not to make a turn to go back to the dressing room. The psychic message being sent indicated to me that I had to leave the platform as well as the building immediately. I ran until I was outside in the street.

Shortly after, all the remaining models, as well as the audience, came running out while screaming in fright. The ceiling in the area where the fashion show was being held had begun collapsing because the store was on fire.

So much for my fifteen minutes of fame!

This next story was a pivotal point in my career choice. This was when I actually decided that my career of clairvoyance was meant to be!

For years, I was doing promotional work. What kind of work is that? I was one of those annoying people who would approach a shopper in a department store asking if he or she wanted a spray of fragrance or, if it were a woman, a cosmetic makeover.

I enjoyed doing that type of work, but the downside of it was that I never went home with money because the week would end with my bringing home shopping bags full of merchandise. I was able to buy many things on layaway and with the use of my employee discount in conjunction with all the sales, the entire experience was not such a good thing for me, from a cash aspect. But, I was very content with that type of employment at that age and time in my life.

Even though I was employed by the company whose items I was promoting, the department store gave me an employee discount because my psychic abilities were of great help to those in charge. Store managers were all appreciative of my talents because with the use of my capabilities, I knew who was going to be shoplifting. While the store detectives were busy looking at who they thought were the obvious shoplifters, I knew the ones who were very discreet about it. It was obvious to me just by looking at the customers who wandered in and out of the store.

This knowledge developed to the point that, because of the fact that so many shoplifters were caught, a famous large department store offered me a job as a store detective. I turned down the offer because of my petite size, fearing that such an occupation would place me in physical jeopardy.

One day, while working as a jewelry model, I was methodically strolling through the store, showing customers the latest samples of what the manufacturer was designing, when suddenly I saw a woman who I was certain was going to shoplift. She was elderly and harmless looking, someone you would least suspect.

I quickly walked over to one of the store detectives standing nearby and told him to pay attention to her. It didn't take this woman long to remove her coat, try on a sweater and then put her coat back on over the sweater. As she attempted to leave the store, she was escorted by security personnel back into the building and taken straight to the office for what would be an appropriate ending to the story. No one would have ever suspected this woman of doing such a crime.

A woman of that age should have known by then that you either pay in money or in consequences!

As the manager of a high-fashion shoe store, I was in charge of all aspects of its operation on a daily basis. This included the store's functions. The wide-ranging tasks encompassed oversight of the store's everyday opening and closing, revenue from sales stock and inventory accountability. I fulfilled the supervisory requirements that were mandated for such a position.

One day, the store received, via a parcel-carrier service, a large shipment of shoes that were packaged in numerous cartons. I enjoyed unpacking the shoe containers because many of the styles fell into the category of my personal fashion taste. This gave me the opportunity to try them on before anyone else had an opportunity to. If I liked the way they looked on my feet, it gave me the advantage of buying them before anyone else was able to.

So, with this in mind, my staff and I began the task of unpacking the cartons. One by one, I broke the seals of the large containers and we all pulled the merchandise out and began to stock the shelves.

There was one box that I kept skipping because I had a feeling about it after touching it. All the cartons looked the same, but I sensed there was something in this particular one that scared me.

When all the boxes were unpacked, the ominous one remained. I didn't relay my feelings to anyone but casually asked the stock boy if he would open and unpack it for me.

I quickly moved to the front of the store in order to begin coordinating the window display. Suddenly, I heard a blood-curdling scream resonating from the rear of the shop. After dropping a pair of new shoes that I was just about to put into the window display, I ran to the back of the shop. My heart was beating quickly and my hunch was that I didn't want to see what was in that carton. But, also knowing that a store manager is responsible for all the store's functions, I needed to be courageous and not cowardly in this case.

There, in the very bottom of the carton, lay a tremendous, dead rat. I never knew that a rodent that size even existed. There had been no odor emanating from it or any other sign of its presence when the carton was closed, but I had known after touching the carton that there was something troublesome inside, and I was right.

This was no *shoe* fly!

One of the many jobs I was happy to have as the years went by was being a home health aide. This position's duties included helping the elderly by chauffeuring them to stores, doctor's appointments and the library as well as paying bills, making phone calls and any other service that was warranted. Essentially, I found it very rewarding.

I had many different patients and each one was special to me. There was one woman who I even had to dance with to make her happy. But, if it lightened and brightened her day, it was good enough for me. She danced with me vigorously. You would never have known she was on in years when she did her dance! This was a fun job!

Tuesday was assigned to one of my patients named Stella. On one particular day, I was writing greeting cards for her and she was in the midst of explaining to me the role each person on the list played in her life and why she was sending each a card.

Suddenly I heard in my ear a hazy sound of a tragedy's immediate aftermath. Someone had just died. The soulful vibes that were speaking to me were almost comparable to someone whispering in my ear to pay attention to what it was saying. It was a skillful revelation that I have had many times over the years. It told me that there was death around me, and it was someone I knew. The message was telling me that it was going to affect me in some capacity.

Of course, I could see that Stella was fine. She was busy picking out the greeting cards she wanted sent out that day. I didn't want her to know about the message of death that I had just received in my psychic knowledge.

The first thought that came into my mind was of my parents, who were somewhat elderly. Not wanting to scare Stella, and at the same time wanting to know who the deceased was, I told her that I needed to leave then and would continue doing our routine on the following visit. She was agreeable, and I left.

After arriving home, I called my parents but tried not to indicate my anxiety concerning their well-being that day. They however, were able to sense my nervousness and asked me what was wrong. By then, they should have realized that this pessimistic behavior was only exhibited when I receive negative psychic messages. But, they didn't, so I explained that there was a bad feeling within me that had created apprehension in my mind. I told them that my inner voice was continuously telling me that there was a sad situation that had already taken place. Not wanting to tell them that there was a feeling of death around me, I quickly hung up the phone, thinking warily that someone with the news would soon call me.

It didn't take long. Two hours later, my phone rang and I knew that this was going to be the answer. The call was from my dear friend Rosalie. She informed me that her only son had committed suicide that afternoon. She cried to me and I tried to comfort her while also crying. I had known her son, Charles, since he was a small child, and I was quite fond of him. It was heartbreaking and so unexpected.

Never forget that we are all connected. You can feel other people's anguish!

I was in Texas, training to be a flight attendant. I was away from home and family, and feeling homesick. The course was twenty-eight days long. On the twenty-sixth day of the course, after school I went directly to a restaurant nearby because hunger and fatigue had taken over my body and my mind. On previous days, I had gone back to my hotel room to change from my business suit to casual attire, but not on that day.

My roommate, Sally, usually went to the hotel bar for happy hour but on that one evening she decided to join me for dinner. She also did not go back to the room.

We went to a popular restaurant next door to the hotel and settled in for a nice dinner. As we were eating, a message was relayed to me through a feeling, telling me that I should quickly return to the hotel because there was an issue that happened or was happening in my room. I immediately called the waitress to my table and requested that she wrap up my food.

My roommate asked me what the problem was and I told her that I had received a feeling of being watched, and I had to leave. Sally didn't understand what was wrong because we had just been conversing about a lot of subjects and all of a sudden, I needed to depart the restaurant. She told me that she opted to go back to the hotel for happy hour instead of going back to the room, but first, she was going to finish her meal.

I ran back to the hotel and upon entering my room noticed that all my belongings were gone. The closet was empty, as were the dresser drawers. I couldn't understand what happened and even though the key fit the lock, I looked again at the room number on the door, thinking that maybe it was the wrong location. With my mind racing about this strange turn of events, I thought of Sally and sprinted back to the restaurant to inform her of the occurrence in our room.

She was still eating when I arrived but, realizing the seriousness of my story, accompanied me back to the hotel. Her inspection revealed that only one of her garments was missing.

We called hotel security and asked that they come to our room. When the head of security asked me to provide a list of all my missing items, he was surprised when I mentioned that my jewelry was gone. He said, "What jewelry?" He asked me where the jewelry had been. I told him that it had been in the inside pocket of my black leather coat. It was then that the realization came to me that he was the thief.

However, he was suggesting that the cleaning lady assigned to the room was responsible for the theft. I had seen the woman several times. She was tall and heavyset. I am petite and even then wore a size two. I knew she wouldn't be interested in my clothes.

I asked the head of security who the left-handed, red-headed woman was in his life. He said it was his wife, and he wanted to know who my source of information was. I told him that I could see her in my mind, wearing my green suede suit and my jewelry. He turned pale and looked stunned.

When the report was completed and hotel security left, I telephoned the local police and asked that they come to the hotel. When a policeman arrived and took my report, he told me that every month he was called to this hotel for robberies. Of course, I couldn't prove that the head of security was the culprit. I had no proof except for my psychic visions.

I was later informed that the police notified the airline that was paying for the room as part of the training program. The airline asked me to take a lie detector test, which I agreed to do and passed. The lie detector test was to prove that I hadn't hidden my clothes for insurance purposes.

The case against me was settled, but I was dismissed from the school because the airline considered me a troublemaker with the hotel with which they had contracted. A month later, the airline went bankrupt and the head of security of the hotel was fired.

Karma?

One morning, I was getting dressed to go to work when the little voice inside my head said, "Don't wear that. Wear something nicer." Not looking to disagree with the message, I changed into a more upscale look.

I went to the store as usual and waited to see why there had been a message sent to me regarding the changing of my clothes that morning. The shoe department where I worked was busy that day and I made myself available to all customers who looked as though they were in need of help.

After walking over to a woman whose face I could not see because she was looking down at a sample shoe on display, I introduced myself and asked if she needed any assistance. She looked up at me and said, "Thanks. I could use some help." To my surprise, the woman looking back at me was a renowned female singer whose tapes I played constantly in my car. Guess who sold her a pair of shoes that day. I did!

She wore them onstage. I saw the scene in my psychic vision!

Many years ago, Zach was employed by a company but, like many other people in his situation, he wished to own his own business. One day, after voicing his frustration to me about not being self-employed, I tried to think about what kind of business he could eventually be in.

Suddenly, as I was listening to him, my palate became very dry. I felt as if my mouth were full of cotton balls. My body seemed as if it were dehydrated and I became very thirsty. In other words, I craved water.

"Zach, I think that you should sell bottled water," I innocently suggested.

"Who would spend money on bottled water when they can get it free from the faucet?" he answered while laughing hysterically.

Well, I don't have to tell anyone about that suggestion. Within a short period of time, bottled water became as common as bottled soda.

Many people are still carrying water when jogging, going to the gym, driving in the car and for any other activity that is performed outside of the house. It even replaced faucet water in the home

Fortunately, Zach realized not too long after my suggestion was made that bottled water was a sign of the times. He started selling cases of bottled water and now he also drinks it.

Water, water everywhere…

Chapter Five

Taking My Chances

Zach and I were leaving Atlantic City, saying goodbye to our money and our friends, who were staying for the evening. Suddenly, a message came through to me saying that we should wait a few hours before departing for home.

When I discussed this psychic premonition with Zach, he asked me why I would want to stay when the time was late and we both needed to work the next day, meaning an early morning wakeup for both of us. I told him that I just felt that we needed to delay our departure for a couple of hours. Of course, he laughed and said, "Maybe you want to stay, but I'm going home." As usual, Zach got his way and we left amid, wishing goodbye and good luck to our friends and telling them that we would see them soon.

We had only driven a few miles when we noticed state troopers out in force as well as roadblocks being put in place. Traffic was at a standstill. The road was closed.

I got out of the car and walked over to one of the parkway police officers and asked him what the problem was. He told me that there was an ongoing forest fire and that no one was going anywhere for at least two hours. Rather than sitting and waiting until the fire was contained, we turned the car around and returned to Atlantic City.

I knew it, and I made sure Zach knew that I knew. "I told you so" was my mantra the whole way back to the hotel. We parked the car, went into the casino and met our friends again.

I told them, "When I said 'see you soon,' I didn't realize it would be this soon!"

One weekend Zach and I went to Atlantic City to do some gambling and have some fun. We looked forward to seeing occasionally the shows with all the popular, well-known performers. It was just a well-deserved weekend away.

Saturday started out uneventfully and by nightfall we were in the casino of the hotel where we were staying. Zach was very comfortably sitting and playing his favorite video poker machine.

I suddenly had a psychic vision of winning, but not at this hotel. The little voice in my head told me which hotel to go to. Of course, there was no way I would miss this opportunity, so I walked over to Zach and told him that we needed to go to a different hotel because of a psychic vision I had just received.

He had no problem with my going to another hotel but was hesitant to go himself because he had put a great deal of money into the machine he was currently playing. He thought that eventually a jackpot would be won right there. Since the location I needed to go to was far from this hotel and it was nighttime, I did not want to go by myself.

Very reluctantly, and after much persuading (also called *nagging*), Zach finally left his machine to take a walk with me. He made the long walk even longer by complaining that the next person who sat down at the machine he had been playing would "luck out." He lectured me, saying that you should only gamble at the hotel you're staying at, etc. I didn't care what he said because I was on my way to winning big at another hotel!

Finally, we arrived at the hotel and after entering the front door decided to get cards that would entitle us to perks that the hotel gave out for free. After filling out the application, the woman at the desk handed me a scratch-off game that she explained could be a winner. All I had to do was pick five boxes out of seventy-five and spell out "money."

I gingerly took out a penny, and the little voice in my head once more came through for me. I was an instant winner, and when I showed the scratch-off ticket to the woman behind the desk, she started to scream. No one had ever won the thousand-dollar prize before, and it was a promotion that had been going on for years. A photographer happily took our picture; the excitement was overwhelming. We were going to be featured in the hotel newsletter and would probably be the talk of the hotel for a long time to come.

We returned to the hotel where we were staying, walking hand in hand, with big smiles on our faces. I was particularly happy because I could say to Zach, "I told you so."

Guess which man I gave half my winnings to? You got it!

I have another startling gambling story. One anniversary, Zach and I decided to go to the Meadowlands racetrack to celebrate. I brought only $20 because I am a sore loser and figured that I would only bet two dollars a race.

As I looked at the program, not knowing one horse from the other, I suddenly had a psychic vision of my cousin Isabel. After looking for a horse with her name in the program and not seeing it, my next option was to find a horse whose name matched the initials of Isabel's first and last name. Sure enough, I found it! I told Zach that I was going to bet the $20 in my purse on this long shot.

He was busy with his own horse picks and wasn't listening to me. He thought that I had only gambled $2 on the horse. When the horse won, he told me that my winnings would be $85, which wasn't bad for $2. However, I told Zach that I bet $20, not $2, and therefore won $850.

Not a bad haul for $20!

Another one of my favorite destiny stories involves a trip to Atlantic City. Zach and I were going there for the weekend and I took out my tarot cards while he was driving.

I told him that not only was this was going to be my lucky day, but I was going to hit the jackpot. Zach was sincerely excited for me and we continued our ride with optimism and anticipation of a great time.

We walked into the casino and since I was feeling lucky, my first stop was going to be in the high-limit area, which was ultimately the place where I made myself comfortable. My usual machines were the quarter ones, but since I knew that providence was watching over me, nothing was going to be wasted on small jackpots.

First I went to a video poker machine. I put $25 into it and the bell rang, telling me and all the other players that I had just won a jackpot of $1,250. This was certainly a good beginning. While waiting for the hostess to bring me my newly found fortune, I went to another machine and put in $25 again. I hit for a royal flush, which paid $20,000. Life was grand!

I then tried a third machine and won $6,500. Knowing when to quit while ahead is the sign of a smart gambler, so I did just that—but not before thanking my anonymous source for giving me the communication that led me to realize my good fortune that day.

When you're winning, you feel like you just can't lose!

Shortly after my mom passed away, I was sitting in a local OTB parlor, thinking about her and her passion for the sport of horse racing. She always had a knack for picking the winner without knowing one horse from the other or even studying the charts. She chose the horse by personal experience, whether it was by the name of the horse, the name of the driver, the number of the horse in the race or the color of the driver's jacket.

I wanted to see if she was around me, so I asked her for a sign. Immediately, the ceiling lights started flashing on and off and finally, they went off altogether. Everyone sitting in the room impatiently waited for the lights to go back on. The emergency beams went on because there were no windows in the room.

I assumed that it must have been raining because that is often the reason for a power failure. I walked carefully through the darkened room and down the long staircase because I wanted to assess the weather conditions outside.

Outdoors, it was bright and sunny. I returned to my seat and waited with Zach and the other patrons for the electricity problem to be resolved. A few minutes later, the lights reappeared. Everyone cheered, and I felt less guilty for almost ruining the afternoon for all the people sitting there. Luckily, no one knew I had been trying to connect with my mom.

I was continuously thinking about what happened and even though I knew that there is no such thing as a coincidence, there was a strong temptation to try it again, just to make sure.

In my mind, I said, "Ma, was that you?" The lights flickered and went off. We were left sitting once more in the dark. Again, I went down the steps, almost not believing my own eyes. The day was still sunny and bright. After returning to the darkened room, I sought the man in charge and asked him if these blackouts happened often. He told me that he had never seen one happen at all.

I guess my mother was playing with all of us that day. She wished that she could be with me, and that was her signal.

That day, I won, and it had nothing to do with money!

Here is another favorite story of mine. You could call it "A Little Too Late."

Zach was sitting in the den and watching horseracing on television. It was the Belmont Stakes. I had no money bet and really wasn't interested in who the winner would be. Zach was going to make a bet by phone and asked me if I wanted to get in on the action. Hesitating, I questioned him regarding how many horses were running. He told me that many horses ran in this race but if I wished, he would read the names to me. After telling him not to bother, I went into the bathroom and began my usual routine of applying make-up.

Suddenly, as I was putting on my lipstick, the case fell from my hand. Now, normally, it wouldn't be a traumatic moment because we all drop things from time to time. But, for some reason, this little lipstick, upon falling, broke the stone statue of a bird that was sitting on the sink vanity. This statue sat approximately two feet from where I was standing. The lipstick hadn't even landed anywhere near where it was dropped. Even for me, this was very strange.

Just then, a vision entered my mind, telling me that one of the horses, whose name was relevant to the statue, was going to win. I yelled out to Zach, "Is there a horse by the name of Stone Bird running?"

He said, "No, but there is a horse by the name of Birdstone."

I replied, "That's the horse that is going to win."

Zach laughed and said, "Too late, the race started and besides, it's not a favorite—it's a long shot."

Moments later, the announcer said, "Birdstone won the Belmont Stakes."

So, not only didn't I have a bet on it, I had a broken statue of a bird made out of stone to remind me!

This next story is one that everyone can relate to because from time to time we all say, "Better them than me!"

On a weekend getaway to Atlantic City, Zach and I were once again on our way to a hotel resort, anxious to get away from the daily routine. Our trip was nothing out of the ordinary, which I was grateful for, and we both looked forward to having a great time.

When we were approximately a mile from our destination, I began to feel anxious and apprehensive. Then, there it was in my mind's eye: I saw broken glass from sliding doors. Where was this scene? My first thought was my home's dining room. But I didn't feel that the broken glass was there.

Was it in the hotel? I tried to meditate on the answer, but it was difficult in the moving car because meditation needs absolute silence with no distractions.

Finally, we reached our destination. We checked in at the hotel and went to our room to get settled. Upon entering the suite, I looked around to see if there were sliding doors to a balcony. There were none. I examined all the mirrors and windows but found nothing.

I walked toward the bathroom and finally discovered what my vision was trying to convey to me. Slivers of glass lay on the tile floor. The glass from the bathtub's sliding doors was broken into so many pieces that they resembled little ice chips.

Upon calling the front desk, I was told that the only other room available was the penthouse, which they were willing to give us for the same price. The management did not mind the expense of the broken glass.

That's more than I can say about how I would feel if it were in my house!

Zach and I attended a Christmas social. It was after midnight, and we were both exhausted. Due to the lateness of the hour and the fact that we were tired, he was urging me to leave.

I did not want to leave because the raffle drawing hadn't taken place yet, and I knew that we possessed the winning ticket. As usual, thinking that I didn't know what I was talking about and was perhaps a little delirious due to my state of fatigue, he asked me how I could know that.

"I smell an aroma of wine, and that is what the prize is," I confidently told him. Again, as usual, we stood there arguing over whether we should leave for home. Happily, I was correct. An hour later, we left the social with a basket of wine.

Instead of being excited about my scent sense and what we won, Zach told me that he could use a drink after staying at the dance an extra hour. He couldn't wait to arrive home and celebrate the end of the dance and the winning of the wine.

Here's to you, Zach. Maybe someday you will believe me!

It was a beautiful summer day and I was feeling lucky. Not wanting to waste the feeling, which really didn't happen too often, Zach and I decided to drive to Orient Point on Long Island. From there, we took a commercial boat across Long Island Sound to Connecticut, where there were several casinos.

On the way to our destination, a vivid visualization suddenly popped into my mind, showing me standing and holding a poster. The vision didn't make any sense until I won $4,000 from a royal flush on a video poker machine. The host of the casino handed me $4,000 in cash and a poster-sized check that displayed the amount. He asked me to hold up the poster so that my picture could be taken for a brochure.

Is this a great country or what?

Zach and I were going to Atlantic City for the weekend and decided that since we were going to be in New Jersey, we would stop at the final resting place of my uncle Lou. When arriving at the cemetery, we found the grave and stood with our heads bent in prayer.

As soon as I closed my eyes, I heard Uncle Lou speaking to me in my psychic hearing (do you think my anonymous source was taking a nap?). He said, "Joy, when you go to the casino, forget about the quarter machines. Head directly to the dollar ones and put in the maximum amount of money you can. You are going to win big!"

When Zach and I slid back into the seats of our car to continue the ride to our destination, I told him about my uncle's message. He laughed while saying, "You and your messages." Not surprised at Zach's answer, but at the same time hesitant to go to the higher-priced slot machines, I debated the point in my mind and then decided to listen to what Uncle Lou had told me. I knew he would never mislead me.

When we arrived at the casino, I went immediately to the dollar slot machines and put in five silver dollars. No win. I put in another five silver dollars and suddenly, there were flashing lights, ringing bells and blowing whistles drawing the attention of everyone in the vicinity. I looked at my machine and there it was: a royal flush. A $4,000 check was on its way. In my mind, I thanked my uncle Lou for the *tip*. I took the money, put it in my wallet and did not gamble any more that day.

Uh…Zach, what was that you were saying about me and my messages?

Zach and I were invited to a "suitcase dinner party." At this event, anyone interested had the opportunity to participate in an unusual raffle. The prize was a weekend getaway. The trip included a chauffeured limousine that would drive the winner to Manhattan, where a luxury hotel suite awaited. As an added bonus, the winner was allowed to bring a guest. It included meals and many other extras to entice people to enter the drawing.

I asked Zach which clothes he wanted to take with him for the weekend. He laughed, saying that there was no need to pack any clothes for the event because it was unlikely that I would win.

After sitting down and meditating on the subject, I realized that I was going to be the winner and again asked Zach which clothes he wanted to bring with him. I knew that in order to qualify for entry into the raffle, each contestant had to open the suitcase he or she had brought to show that it contained clothing. An empty suitcase was not acceptable. Again, he told me not to bother because there was no way that I would win.

I quickly packed the suitcase with my clothes and toiletries and even included a camera. If Zach didn't trust my judgment, he would have to wear the same clothes that he was wearing to the dinner for the entire weekend.

Well, by now you must know the ending. My raffle ticket was drawn. I won! I was fully prepared, but guess who wasn't. Zach begged the chauffeur to take him home for a change of clothes. The driver refused, saying that it was against the rules and that the regulations of the contest stated that the winner had to be taken directly to Manhattan to start the weekend. Zach had to wear the clothes on his back the entire time.

Zach, aren't you a believer yet?

Chapter Six

Personal Things

My parents were planning to go to the movies one afternoon and of course, they included me. It was a rainy day and the movie sounded like fun.

We were all sitting in the car in the garage, and my father turned the key in the ignition. I said to my father in a panic, "Don't back out of the garage now."

"Why not?" he asked.

"Because Boots is under the car and I don't want her to die," I cried. Boots was the family cat, and I was very fond of her. I didn't see her, but I could feel her presence behind the tire.

My father got out of the vehicle to look underneath. He gave a cursory glance, said he did not see her and sat back down in the seat of the car. He looked at me, smiled and promised that he would back out slowly. Still, I yelled, "No, don't!"

My father, who was obviously getting impatient with me, said, "We are leaving now because if we don't, we'll miss the beginning of the movie." He slowly backed the car out. Just as the tires started to roll, we heard Boots cry in pain. My father had run the car over her. She had been sitting behind the rear tire. He stopped the car, jumped out quickly and saw her lying there.

I was hysterical. I yelled, "I knew it, I knew it!"

My mother was angry with my father, saying, "You should have checked more thoroughly for Boots. Now look what happened."

Needless to say, the movie was not on anyone's mind anymore. We gently put Boots into the car and then drove to the local animal hospital. After examining her carefully, the veterinarian told us that my precious cat Boots had to be put to sleep. She could not be saved because of multiple injuries. I was heartbroken.

My mother, trying to console me, went to the local store to buy me a toy stuffed gray cat to make up for my loss. I named it Boots. But no cat in the world would ever replace the real Boots. I was left with only a pretend cat to take her place.

Throughout my life, I have had many different feline friends and I have loved them all. In fact, all the pets I've owned have been precious to me, and each has given me unconditional love.

Wouldn't it be nice if people were like that?

Another cat story that I think about often happened while I was sitting in church, waiting for the service to start. I was seated next to a woman I had never seen before. She introduced herself as Lucille and as we sat together we discussed the weather and other trivial subjects. Slowly, the rest of the members of the congregation filtered in to find their seats.

While sitting there, I noticed that Lucille appeared very distraught and anxious, and was dabbing her eyes with a handkerchief. Thinking about the possibility of calming her down, I closed my eyes for a moment, trying to get a picture of what was bothering her.

In my mind's eye, an abundance of laundry in a basket sat in front of an electric clothes dryer. I could see Lucille throwing in some wet wash from the basket. When she turned her back to get a fabric softener sheet, a cat that was sitting next to the clothes dryer jumped in without Lucille noticing it. Since the laundry was white and the cat was white, there was no obvious sign of anything being wrong.

Lucille, not realizing the perilous position that her pet had placed itself in, proceeded to turn on the dryer. The cat, needless to say, died.

I turned to Lucille and told her to stop blaming herself for the death of her cat. She looked at me in shock. "How do you know about "Snowball?"

I told her of the psychic abilities I possessed and the way the whole incident regarding Snowball had played out in my mind. I gave her an account of what had happened to my cat Boots, which was very similar.

I promised to send her a copy of a consoling pet poem that described a wonderful place where creatures went when they died. I have always found it to be a very calming piece of writing and recommend it highly to anyone who grieves the loss of an animal.

Several weeks later, I met Lucille again in church. She thanked me for the poem, which I had mailed to her, and told me that it was a tremendous help and comfort to read.

The loss of a pet can be just as painful as the loss of a person!

I have one more cat story, and this one is really phenomenal.

Not so many years ago, Zach and I were the proud owners of three cats. Their names were Buddy, Cleo and Beth. We spent many happy hours playing with these adorable creatures, each of which had its own personality and character traits.

One day, Zach and I decided to buy a cat tree house for them. It was seven feet tall and weighed over 200 pounds. It had carpeted tunnels for them to play in and different levels from which they could jump. All three cats played in their little condominium every day.

As any pet lover knows, the deaths of these cats were devastating. Needless to say, I miss them very much.

One day, I was thinking about them and went into the bathroom where they had often liked to gather when they weren't in the cat tree house. I closed the door and thought that maybe I would be able to see them all together one more time.

After sitting down on the floor, I shut my eyes for thirty seconds and asked the powers that be for a chance to see my departed pets that I had loved so dearly. When I opened my eyes, out came all three of them—Buddy leapt down from the bathtub, Beth came out from under the vanity and Cleo jumped down from the sink. Beth climbed into my lap and sat with me just as she used to when she was living in this dimension. I stroked her, as well as the other two, while crying from happiness at seeing them. This whole episode lasted approximately three minutes. Then, they disappeared as quickly as they had come.

That night, while getting undressed, I noticed that my black turtleneck sweater, which I had just removed from the plastic dry-cleaning bag that morning, had cat hair on it even though there were no live cats in my house.

Was it proof that it really happened? I'm a believer!

I was standing on line, waiting to pay for the food I was purchasing at the supermarket. When my turn came, I sought to help the cashier and began to bag all of my groceries. Before paying, there was, in my psychic hearing, a little voice telling me to beware of the cashier. It warned me that she was going to give me back the wrong amount of change.

The food bill amounted to $80.50. I gave the cashier two $50 bills and the exact change that was owed. The cashier put it into the drawer and handed me back two $5 bills. I waited for her to also give me a $10 bill. When she didn't, I told her of her error. She insisted that she had given me a $10 bill when she had handed me the two fives.

I called the manager over to where I was standing and explained the situation. He was very understanding and told me that he would know soon enough. He opened the cash register drawer, counted the money and then handed me the extra $10 due me.

He was very angry with the cashier and told her that she could leave.

My anonymous source was saying, "Buyer, beware!"

This next story is about something that every woman who is a shoe lover can appreciate!

One Thanksgiving Day, Zach and I went to the Macy's parade, which is held every year in Manhattan. We stood there and watched all the festivities. The crowds were enormous and the noise, excitement and camaraderie were something special to be seen and heard.

As we watched the floats go by, Zach turned to me and said, "You seem distracted. Is everything alright?"

I responded to him by closing my eyes, trying to visualize why I had a feeling that I needed to return home. I was positive that there was something wrong inside my apartment, but not sure what the problem was. I thought carefully, going through a checklist of all the things I normally did before leaving to go out. This included the usual rituals such as checking the stove, turning off the lights, lowering the thermostat and locking the door. I was sure that I remembered to activate the burglar alarm.

"Enjoy the day," Zach said. "You're always worried. Everything is fine."

Suddenly, while I was looking down at my shoes, my feelings turned to dismay, which made me say, "I should have worn my old shoes, not my designer ones. These are going to be ruined!"

Zach looked at me with curiosity. "Why are you worrying about your shoes? It's not going to rain."

"I don't know," I replied.

After being out most of the day, we finally returned home. Upon opening the front door, Zach and I discovered water throughout the apartment. It had soaked through the carpet and destroyed all the Christmas gifts on the floor in the closet.

Another family lived on the floor above us, but upon inspection of the ceiling and wall, we ascertained that our upstairs neighbor's apartment was not the source of the flooding. We searched the entire apartment, looking for the cause of this disaster, but it eluded us.

After further speculation of the probable flood starting place, we returned to look in the master bedroom and the answer to our problem was finally located: a leak in the waterbed was the reason for this latest catastrophe.

My shoes, which I had worried about at the parade, were safely dry in the building's hallway because I had removed them as soon as we had opened the front door and seen the massive puddle of water in the foyer.

I was angry at myself for not listening to my own inner voice and coming home sooner. If I had trusted my intuition, there wouldn't have been such water damage.

No psychic, good or otherwise, would have wanted to be in my shoes that day!

Here is another story about shoes! I certainly will not forget this anecdote and you won't either!

One evening, while I was preparing to go to a psychic fair in a nearby hotel, a vision of Cinderella and her shoes came into my mind. I could not stop thinking about the shoes. They were so beautiful, but what did they have to do with me? *Why am I thinking about Cinderella's shoes?* was the thought that continuously went through my mind.

The fair wasn't anything out of the ordinary and at closing time I gathered up all my belongings and headed toward the parking lot. I always get a little nervous walking alone to my car in the evening. I had almost arrived when a man appeared out of nowhere. He politely asked me to stop walking, which I did. After opening his wallet, he offered me four $100 bills. While promising that he wouldn't hurt me, he requested that I give him my shoes. In return, he committed to give me the money he was holding in his hand.

As much as I would have liked the money, it just sounded too weird to me. I told him that my shoes were not for sale. Seeing that this was not going to be an easy transaction, he then offered me an extra $100. At that point I told him that no amount of money was acceptable.

As we were talking, I slowly inched toward my car, trying to get away from this odd man. I unlocked the door and quickly slid into the seat of my vehicle but was increasingly fearful that he would follow me home.

Thank goodness for my car racing experience. That night, it proved to be an asset to me. He followed me when I left the parking lot, but he was unable to catch up to me. I lost sight of him somewhere on the parkway.

When I was getting undressed for bed that night, I remembered the Cinderella's shoe vision from earlier in the evening and laughed out loud. I never returned to that hotel, nor did I ever see that man again. But I still have those shoes and, more importantly, my dignity!

What would you have done?

It was moving day and Zach and I were excited about our new home. We were anticipating the decorative effect of the newly ordered furniture and continued to assess what other items we were going to need for this next chapter of our lives.

That night, we got into bed with a healthy tiredness, the kind you get after a job is well done or a decision is well thought out. It didn't take us long to fall asleep thanks to the hectic day that we had experienced.

Suddenly, I was awakened by music—a chorus of singers. Thinking that maybe Zach had left the radio on, I quickly got out of bed and went looking for the source of the entertainment. To my surprise, I couldn't find any radios, televisions or other music players turned on. The cause of the passionate singing was really puzzling to me.

The house in which we were now living was in a brand-new development and subsequently, not all the units had been sold. No one lived in the dwellings on either side of us, which prevented me from blaming this enthusiastic performance on a noisy neighbor who had forgotten to shut off his radio or television.

Upon making inquiries the next day, I found out that all these new homes had been built on the land where a gospel church had previously stood, and I had been hearing the music from its choir. After that, I heard the same vocalizations every night at bedtime. This was difficult to live with when it was time to wind down and go to sleep, so I had to purchase a machine that made white noise to drown out the sound of the chorus.

As much as the melodies were beautiful to listen to, it just wasn't the lullaby that I needed to end the day!

This is a story all women will be able to relate to. When you go to someone else's house what do you do with your handbag?

While in the car on the way to a dinner party given by a friend I had known since high school, Zach handed me $160 for groceries to be purchased the following week. I had asked him for the money earlier while we were home, but he had forgotten to give it to me. Not anxious to take the money at that particular time, I asked him to hold on to it until later. But Zach said that I should take it then or he would probably forget about it again. Reluctantly, I took it.

When we arrived at the dinner party, there was another couple already there who were dear friends of the host and hostess. We had first met this couple many years earlier. After sitting and chatting in the living room for a while, we were soon called into the dining room by the hostess for an anticipated lovely dinner.

After we had begun eating, an anxious feeling came over me regarding the money in my purse. Excusing myself from the table, I went into the living room to retrieve my handbag and bring it back with me into the dining room. Unfortunately, that area of the house was quite small and there was actually no spot on the floor or anywhere else to put my pocketbook, so I rested it on my lap.

Upon seeing this, Zach said, "There is no one in the living room. It will be safe there. What are you doing?" He was becoming increasingly annoyed with me. He pointed to the living room and said, "This is a private home, not a public place. Put it back in there."

Not wanting to create an embarrassing spectacle in front of the guests and the hosts, I went back to the living room and put my purse on the floor, between the couch and the end table. My desire was to hide it and believe me, I was not happy to leave it there.

As soon as I returned to the dining room, the uneasiness came over me again. Even though there were no small children in the house and everyone was accounted for in the dining room, I continued to feel an impending problem. My usual symptoms of sweating and trembling were starting to appear.

Dinner was finally over and the hostess decided to serve dessert and coffee in the dining room, which meant that no one was going back into the living room. But by that point, I was positive that my wallet needed my undivided attention.

After excusing myself to go to the rest room, which was merely a reason to walk through the living room, I deliberately left the table to see what was happening with my purse. No one seemed to suspect my uneasiness.

Upon entering the living room, I noticed that my handbag wasn't on the floor where I had placed it. Instead, it was on the other side of the room, on top of the sofa. My first thought was that the hostess had moved it because there was a dog in the house and she didn't want my handbag to be in harm's way. (Ironically, I felt safer in the house because there was a dog, which would have barked if an intruder sneaked in. But obviously, it wasn't comforting enough for me because the intense feelings stayed with me.)

I then observed that my purse was open, as was my wallet. What was I to do? Not wanting to embarrass my friend, her husband or the other guests, I called to Zach, telling him that he should come into the living room.

Of course, he refused to come because he was in the middle of a conversation and wanted to finish giving his opinion on the matter being discussed. In a manner that no one could decipher as anything but panic, I yelled once more for him to come in. But again, he refused.

The host, realizing from my tone of voice that something was terribly wrong, came into the living room and saw me standing next to the couch with my open, empty wallet.

When I told him about the situation, he immediately took out his wallet from his pants pocket, opened it and without hesitation withdrew $160 from it. He didn't even question my honesty regarding the missing money. He then went on to explain in a very subdued voice that his stepson, Brian, would periodically sneak into the house to steal money and jewelry. The story unfolded that this young man had a drug problem and was very desperate to get money for his addiction. Of course, this was not something that his mother and stepfather were proud of, and therefore they did not divulge this information to anyone, including friends.

They had changed all the locks on the doors but today, the front door had been left open because there were guests in the house. The dog knew Brian and had not barked.

The evening ended with no one except the host and myself knowing the story of the missing money. I no longer carry money in my wallet when visiting anyone's house, to avoid another awkward situation.

Anonymous source, I know you were trying to warn me! Why does everything happen to me?

My housekeeper, Jeanette, was planning to marry her boyfriend, Peter, after dating him for many years. Since I had known her for a substantial number of years, she asked my opinion of her plans.

I closed my eyes for a vision and then, unfortunately, had to tell her that I could see Peter going into a hotel with another woman. My vision was definitely giving me a feeling that he was dishonest. There was sneaky behavior going on without Jeanette's knowledge. He was leading a double life.

Upon hearing this, Jeanette went home and sought possession of Peter's cell phone bill. After checking the numbers that had been dialed from that phone, she discovered an unfamiliar one being called daily.

Jeanette called the number and confronted the other woman, who did not know that Jeanette even existed in Peter's life.

You know the saying about a woman scorned? Talk about furious!

For several years, I had a personal trainer named Jennifer who came to my home three times a week. She was a lovely young girl who worked very hard to help me achieve my goal of being physically fit.

Upon awaking one morning when we were scheduled for a session, I felt the need for her to stay home. I had no idea why, but my judgment told me that she needn't come on that particular day. It was almost a feeling that I had to let her know that it would be alright if she skipped the appointment.

After reaching for the telephone and dialing her number, I realized that there should be a reason for her not to come. Not knowing what to say but calling her anyway seemed ridiculous, but I did it. As usual, the reason would show itself.

Her mother answered the phone and when I asked to speak to Jennifer, she told me that she was still sleeping. Suddenly, I realized that the woman to whom I was speaking sounded very upset. Without knowing if it was appropriate for me, a stranger, to intrude on her thoughts and possibly her problems, I hinted to her that she sounded upset about something.

She told me that Jennifer did not yet know, but her dog, a dear family pet for many years, had passed away during the night. Jennifer's mother was very anxious about the relaying of this sad news to her daughter. But, she did tell me that it was a very remote chance that Jennifer would be able to function as my trainer that day.

Her mom was absolutely correct. Jennifer had spent many sessions telling me how much she adored her pet. She carried pictures of the dog and was always anxious to return home in order to play with him.

I was given my reason for Jennifer having to stay home that day, and it was a very sad one. If only I could have taken away the pain!

Whether it was from my occupation of reading tarot cards or the severe beating from the home invasion or perhaps both, my back was starting to bother me a great deal.

One day, I noticed a sign indicating that a doctor, a back specialist, was practicing near my home. I pondered visiting him, changing my mind and then changing it back. Should I go or wait? Maybe the pain would go away by itself. I was in such agony, I decided that nothing would be lost and possible something could be gained if I went to his office. I was desperate for help. I decided to seriously think about it.

Several days later, I was contemplating going to the emergency room at the local hospital because my back pain was so severe. I was almost passing out from the agony of the spasms.

In an instant decision, I called the doctor's office that I had noticed several days earlier and begged the receptionist to let me come in to see the doctor right away. She said that his schedule was full but since I was suffering to such an immense degree, she would make room for me. I quickly got dressed and rushed to his office.

When I entered the waiting room, to my chagrin I found a room filled with patients. I questioned whether my pain tolerance would hold long enough for me to wait. The back spasms were getting more and more excruciating. The other patients, seeing my discomfort, urged the receptionist to let me go in before them. They were all just very kind and compassionate people.

Thinking and hoping that maybe it would work out for me, I filled out the necessary insurance forms and, to my surprise, was immediately ushered into an examination room. Soon after, the doctor entered. He walked over to the chair in which I was sitting and said, "Talk to me." He could see from the grimace on my face that I was feeling pain. He then told me to lie down for an examination and that hopefully, he would be able to help me get through the agony that I was experiencing.

Doing as he requested, I got onto the table and lay facedown. He began to work on relieving the stinging sensation in my back, and I began to feel much better.

Suddenly, there was the smell of burning candle wax. This indicated to me that it was the doctor's birthday. I said to him, "It's a shame that you have to work on your birthday."

He was startled by my remark. I couldn't see his facial reaction, but there was a long silence. He said, "How did you know it's my birthday? I didn't tell anyone. My receptionist doesn't even know." He was clearly fascinated.

He asked me what gifts he would get. I told him, "Let it be a surprise for you."

The massage that he gave relaxed me, and I honestly believe that my intuitive powers were acute at that time. I had a "light bulb" moment.

When I left the office, I was feeling better, and the doctor was still wondering how this new patient discovered that it was his birthday. He kept shaking his head in wonderment.

Years later, I met him and his wife in a restaurant lobby while Zach and I were waiting to be seated. He said "hello" to me and then turned to his wife and said, "That's the patient I was telling you about who knew that it was my birthday."

When someone remembers one of my psychic messages, it's a *present* to my gift!

Another example of receiving a message but not knowing what it pertained to is as follows:

Once, I woke up in the middle of the night to get a drink of water and as I walked into the kitchen I received an urgent psychic message: an image of pots and bowls filled up with water. As tired as I was, I knew that to ignore this psychic picture would be a mistake, so while in the kitchen I opened the cabinets and pulled out all my pots and bowls, along with any other vessels that would hold water. After the containers were full, I placed them neatly on the counter and stove while wondering why they were needed to begin with.

This seemed to be such an odd thing to do, and it only added to the fact that there weren't any logical reasons for my actions. It even had me baffled. But, I have learned never to question the messages.

I went back to bed. In the morning, the phone rang early, waking me up. The call was from a neighbor who asked me if I had any running water in the apartment, because she had none. When I tested the faucet in my kitchen sink, it had no running water.

Later that afternoon, I was told by a different neighbor that a pipe had broken in the building and the landlord was forced to shut off all the water without any advance notice. I was thankful to have gotten the message the previous night.

Anonymous source, thanks for the warning. You make me feel so smart!

PART TWO

Reading for Others

I am devoting the next part of this book to the many wonderful and interesting people with whom I have crossed paths and spoken during my many years as a tarot card reader and clairvoyant.

I originally met many of these clients at psychic fairs held in various hotels, catering halls and other public places in New York City and Long Island. Another venue for my psychic readings has been psychic parties sponsored by individuals in their residences, where family and friends were invited.

I have also done telephone readings in my own home, which do not provide me with a physical view of the person but the voice, along with the name and date of birth, can give me the information that is needed just as well. Lastly, I have appeared on television and spoken on talk radio, where callers have asked me specific questions about their lives.

Many of the stories I have heard during my career are not only fascinating but sad. I have had clients seriously discuss what they perceive as messages from dreams, feelings or other sources. Unfortunately, they are afraid to share any of these communications with family or friends due to the risk of being shunned or labeled mentally unsound.

Another issue to be addressed concerns those individuals who think that I have some uncanny power to make things happen. I cannot crawl into any young woman's mind with the goal of persuading a reconnection to a previous boyfriend or psychically motivate a young man to leave his current significant other to return to his girlfriend from the past. And, most importantly, I don't possess the ability to put a curse on any man or woman who has cheated on a spouse.

I explain to all who ask for such services that I do not control any person's destiny. Many of our lives' happenings are not even controlled by our own power, and I am just the messenger who reads what is sent to me. The final decisions regarding any person's future are determined by whatever ultimate force exists and each individual person.

Another frequent request that I refuse to entertain is actual psychic spying on family, friends or even neighbors. Many clients aren't as interested in their own existences as they are in other people's lives. I will not provide information about anyone unless it is relevant to the person asking the question.

Also very common to my trade are people who question me regarding their loved ones who have passed over to the other side. They ask if these deceased souls are happy, healthy and safe. Many want to know if any beloved spirits are perhaps watching over all of those who were left behind.

Sometimes, I can actually see the beings with whom an individual is requesting contact. But there are also times when an entity comes through whom the person was not expecting or with whom he or she does not want to interact. Again, it is not in my power to control the entities appearing in my communications because we are all connected and I am not the controlling energy.

Financial dealings are a frequent area of concern. There are many who are curious as to whether a new business venture would be lucrative enough to attempt. Should a job be changed or a salary raise be requested? Is a move to another city or state the right solution? All of these questions are important for those individuals in a quandary, looking for answers.

Lastly, the most common inquiries are in regard to future events and predictions. Many want to know but are afraid to ask because no one wants to hear about negative forecasts, if that will be the case.

I must also mention that there are those who try to trick me by asking questions that they know cannot be answered because the bases of the inquiries are false. To this day, I can't understand why people would want to waste their or my time with questions that are meaningless. If I haven't an answer for them, I just say that I have no response because the event or story never happened or isn't possible. I have always considered myself an honest and trustworthy person and hope that others see me as a person with those characteristics.

This is a vocation that many find fascinating and as you read many of these stories, you might relate to them or even recognize your own story, which is possibly very similar. All lives seem different and at the same time, they very often seem the same. I have changed the names, but the psychic phenomena are true.

As you read, it will probably become obvious that there are many subjects on the minds of the people inhabiting our sphere of existence. I have done many, many psychic interpretations in my long career, and I want to give you samples from actual readings evidencing what people are experiencing in their lives. These excerpts might be short or long, but they all have one thing in common: they are true and informative communications from outside of the world we know and in which we live. These messages are given to me by an unidentified informant and are from a location that I cannot specifically identify.

You should realize one important fact while reading the upcoming portion of my book: every person who has ever inhabited this earth, regardless of race, religion, age, health, gender, intelligence or financial situation, can be read clairvoyantly if that individual wants to be. This means to me that all people are equal and no person is less important than anyone else…to my anonymous source who resides in an unknown place.

Chapter Seven

How Did You Know That?

One of my clients, Tammy, was a young married woman who was a great believer in metaphysics. She considered me a very close confidant and called me quite often for psychic readings. Unfortunately, her relationship with her parents was strained, so she stayed emotionally close to me.

One day, Tammy telephoned me with the happy news that she and her husband, Jerry, were expecting a baby. Of course, I was excited for her and predicted that she was going to be the mother of a little girl. The year was 1972; in those days, expectant parents didn't know the gender of their baby until the blessed event occurred. Tammy was ecstatic, telling me that she was going to waste no time in accruing a wardrobe for her little "princess."

The months went by quickly, and Tammy called me often to update me on the progress of her pregnancy. One Sunday morning, the telephone rang early and upon answering it, I heard Tammy's voice on the other end of the line. She told me that she was leaving for the hospital and asked me if I would come and wait for the birth with Jerry.

Because of the numerous readings that I had done for this baby during the last several months, I felt as if my presence at the hospital would be logical and helpful. I told Tammy that it would be my pleasure to go and wait with the soon- to-be father. Quickly, I got dressed and hurried to meet Jerry to await the birth of the baby.

After arriving at the hospital, I was directed to the maternity area and looked for Jerry. I found him sitting amid a large crowd in the waiting room. We both spoke excitedly regarding the impending birth as we waited for the news.

While sitting there, Jerry alerted me to the fact that the labor rooms were quite busy and that Tammy's doctor told him that more than one expectant mother was being put into each delivery room, due to the amount of patients and the shortage of delivery rooms.

Two hours later, a nurse came out of the labor and delivery room area and, with a big smile on her face, announced that Tammy and her baby boy were doing just fine. I was stunned when I heard this announcement. Knowing that there had been a mistake, I naturally felt the need to see Tammy as soon as possible, to tell her.

Shortly after this unexpected news, Jerry and I went into Tammy's room. Finding her still sleepy from the anesthetic that had been given to her, we both stood there quietly, waiting for her to wake up and become somewhat alert.

Tammy's roommate, who was sitting up in bed, seemed positively thrilled that she had given birth to a baby girl. She informed us that she had shared the delivery room with Tammy and gleefully also told us that she had a little boy at home who was three years old. Now she had a son and a daughter.

Suddenly, one of the nurses entered the room and wanted to speak to Tammy and her husband. Since Tammy still had her eyes closed, the nurse addressed her question to Jerry, asking him if he wanted to have his son circumcised. In an instant, Tammy opened her eyes and said, "Joy, you said that I was going to have a baby girl."

I told Tammy that she definitely did have a girl and that the babies' bracelets had been switched in the delivery room due to the overcrowding and confusion. Understandably, Tammy became very upset. She attempted to get out of her bed, but Jerry and I told her to stay where she was. The nurse, who was still standing in the room, waiting for the answer regarding the circumcision, was adamant that the baby in question was Tammy's and no one else's.

In spite of all of our pleading and yelling, Tammy got out of her bed and, holding on to the wall, walked down the hall to the nursery. She found the nurses' desk and insisted to the head nurse that she wanted a blood test done to determine if the newborn baby boy was hers. The nurse was very angry that Tammy had gotten out of bed so soon after the birth. She scolded her and told her that there was no question regarding who this baby's mother was.

Tammy refused to listen to anything that the nurse said and replied that in no way would she consider returning to her room until the nurse agreed to give the baby a blood test. I was very upset about this whole situation because I knew without a doubt that Tammy's roommate's baby really belonged to Tammy.

By now, you probably know the ending. Tammy and her baby daughter went home five days later. The roommate was disappointed, and the hospital administrator was relieved that the situation would not turn into a massive lawsuit twenty years later.

Maybe a psychic should be assigned to every pregnant woman!

Theresa called me when I was on a television show, wanting to know where her wedding album was. She could not find it. In addition, she wanted to know how her deceased parents were doing.

After closing my eyes for concentration on the matter at hand, I was able to answer both of Theresa's questions. The first thing that I became aware of was that she was a believer in metaphysics, because the information came so easily to me.

First, I informed her that the wedding album was on the top shelf in the storage room. Theresa told me that she had already looked in that part of her house. But the voice in my head would not be stilled. It kept telling me that she should look again. So, after I relayed the message to her, Theresa walked with her portable phone to the storage room. Finally, after exploring the area once more, she found it on the top shelf, caught between a ledge and the wall.

Regarding her second question, I was able to inform Theresa that her parents were "around and watching her." I was able to obtain the fact that her mother, Mona, was happy with the note that Theresa had written and slipped into the pocket of Mona's burial dress.

Then, Theresa asked me if I knew what was written on the note. Without any hesitation, I told her that the paper was a communication to her mom that Theresa was pregnant and that the baby girl would be named Mona.

I also added to the reading the fact that during much of Mona's life, she had a weight problem. She fought a continuous battle to lose the excess pounds because she had quite a passion for desserts. Theresa confirmed what I was saying and was very excited about the messages.

Then, Theresa asked me about her father. After explaining to her that my psychic hearing sense was telling me that her father's name was John, I also had to add that he was concerned about her reckless driving. Theresa laughed. Excitedly, she validated to me that her father's name was John and that she had been stopped recently by a police officer and given a traffic ticket for speeding.

I continued my reading by telling Theresa that she possessed John's shoeshine kit, which was currently being stored on a closet shelf, also in the storage room. Theresa assured my accuracy for this part of the reading by saying that her father had always taken great pride in his appearance and never left the house without first shining his shoes.

I was receiving more communications meant for Theresa. I repeated what I heard concerning her struggle to quit smoking. I told Theresa that Mona and John were very proud that she was able to free herself of the habit.

"What were the coins about?" I asked. Theresa told me that whenever she felt the urge to have a cigarette, she would put coins in a jar. Within a relatively short time, she had accumulated $200.

At this point, the television producer interrupted the reading to ask Theresa if I had ever spoken to her prior to this phone call. Theresa informed the producer that she had never before spoken to me and actually had been browsing through the television channels and chanced upon this one—it had looked interesting.

You just have to believe!

Marisa called me for a phone reading. I closed my eyes to meditate and found my vision focused at a zoo, with the kangaroos. My eyes wouldn't leave the pouch of the animal, which indicated to me that Marisa was pregnant.

She confirmed her upcoming motherhood and told me that she was in her second month of pregnancy, and had just returned from the doctor's office. I asked her who Ashley was and she squealed in delight that her new baby would be called that name if it were a girl.

Seven months later, my mail contained a birth announcement welcoming baby Ashley into the world!

One day, at a psychic fair, a lovely young lady by the name of Alyssa sat down at my table. After we spoke briefly, I asked her if she liked bread. She laughed and told me that she worked in a bread factory and baked plenty of it.

I then told her that I was hearing the name Melissa. Could she relate to that? I was feeling that it was a close relative, perhaps, a sister. She happily volunteered the fact that her twin sister was named Melissa and that this sibling was her best friend.

While we were on the subject of names, I told Alyssa that I was being told psychically that her legal name wasn't Alyssa. She revealed to me that Alyssa was really her middle name. She used it because she didn't like the first name that her parents had given her.

After telling her that I felt that she wasn't giving me the whole story, she gave me more of the details. Her given name was Rosalie. She didn't want to use it because her father had at one time had an extramarital affair with a woman by that name, shortly after Alyssa's birth. Since her mother would get upset whenever hearing or saying the name Rosalie, she began calling Rosalie Alyssa, the middle name.

You cannot fool my anonymous source. It knew that Alyssa was not her real first name and the reason why she wasn't being called by the name Rosalie!

After meeting Gayle for the first time at a psychic fair, I was seeing dollar signs—even though there was a feeling that no money was being spent. My inner voice was counting and sorting money. I asked her why these messages were coming through to me. She explained that she was the bookkeeper for a car dealership.

When I mentioned someone around her whose name began with the letter D, Gayle informed me that her husband's name was Danny. When she said his name, I felt a pain in my left foot, which was telling me that Danny had a physical issue occurring in that area. Gayle began to scream in amazement because I knew about the heel spur in Danny's left foot. She told me that this problem had been bothering him for quite a while.

I can literally feel someone else's pain even if that person isn't in front of me!

MaryAnn and Gavin came for a reading together. I had the feeling just from looking at them that someone was stealing from their home on a regular basis. When I revealed this piece of news to them, they looked puzzled and each quickly stated that nothing seemed to be missing. Before they finished their explanations, I advised them both to be more aware of what was happening in their immediate surroundings.

Gavin was totally dismissive of what I was suggesting and wanted to change the subject. MaryAnn chose to continue speaking about the feeling I had in my mind. She told me that both she and Gavin had jobs and were not home during the day. Again, she stated that there were no indications that anything had been stolen.

I told them that the thing that was being taken was some type of service for which they were actively paying. Both MaryAnn and Gavin appeared confused; their minds raced to figure out what was being taken from them. I suggested that one of them leave work early one day to see what was happening at the house.

A week later, Gavin called me on the phone to tell me that he had decided to go home for lunch instead of eating at the office, which he usually did. Upon pulling his car into the driveway, he noticed that there was an electric wire plugged into an outdoor outlet on his house.

After following the wire, which was a series of connected extension cords leading to the house next door, he found a contractor inside who was working on the new home. The carpenter, Gavin continued, who was in the midst of using power tools to finish off the framing of a door, looked up when Gavin walked in but then went back to what he was doing.

Gavin was incensed at what he was seeing. He inquired why a wire was connected to the outdoor electrical outlet on the house next door. The carpenter stopped working and said to Gavin, "My boss didn't give me a generator, so I thought that the neighbor wouldn't mind if I used his electrical service."

Gavin identified himself as the neighbor and then stated that he minded very much. "It is my electricity being used and if you want to use the outlet on my house, you will have to pay for the wattage being generated."

After finding out the name and phone number of the builder, Gavin called the gentleman on the phone. The builder told him that the carpenter was a subcontractor who was supposed to bring his own generator. Gavin was so angry after that conversation that he began to close the circuit-breaker switch to the outside outlet before he and MaryAnn went to work in the morning.

Several weeks later, Gavin called me again to say that the electrical bill was considerably lower than it had been the previous month. He thanked me for the warning and was happy to talk about the subject now. He finished the phone call by asking, "By the way, how did you know about this?"

My anonymous source knew all about what was going on!

The next story is similar and also quite common. You might even be a victim of this scam.

Blanche sat down at the fair and immediately I could see that although she was quite elderly, she was mentally sharp and very well aware of everything and everyone around her.

My first comment to Blanche concerned where she lived. The feeling that I was receiving was that her residence was in an apartment complex. Blanche answered in the affirmative. I informed her that there was a theft being committed by her next-door neighbor. She told me that she was retired and rarely left her home. She continued to tell me that when she did go out shopping or on other errands, nothing was moved, touched or out of place when she returned.

I then informed her that Ralph, her neighbor, had gone into the basement and hooked Blanche's television cable wire onto his television wire in order to get free cable service.

Blanche left my table at the fair with a mission in mind: to find out if the reading I had given her was accurate. I was certain that this woman would be vigilant regarding finding out of the truth of the matter.

Blanche called me several days later and confirmed my reading by telling me that she had gone to see Ralph and asked him to show her a recent cable bill for the sake of comparison to hers. She told him a story about being afraid that the cable company was overcharging her. Ralph appeared very nervous when she posed this request. He told her that his wife, Joan, handled all the bills and that he had no idea where she kept them.

Later on in the day, Blanche saw Joan return from shopping and stopped her in the street. Blanche asked Joan if she could see the monthly cable bill. Joan told Blanche that Ralph took care of all the bill paying and that she didn't know where to look for it.

It was then that Blanche decided to call the cable company and inform the business office of her suspicions. The company sent a representative to investigate the situation. Upon inspection of the premises, it was found that Blanche's neighbors were indeed sharing her cable service and therefore stealing.

Talk about nerve!

Jill was a waitress who lived in upstate New York. She called me for a reading by telephone after getting my name from her cousin, who lived near me.

I told her that I was seeing a hair salon and was hearing the name Michael. Jill said that Mike was her husband and that he was a hairstylist.

For some reason, I was seeing a vision of costumes starting to unfold in my mind. They weren't the kind you would see in a Broadway show, but rather the scary type. This was telling me that Halloween was her preferred holiday. I reported to Jill what I was seeing.

"Yes, Halloween is definitely my favorite holiday. It is the one I look forward to every year," she said with a hesitant laugh.

"I'm also seeing tattoos on your body. Is this correct?" I asked.

"Do you have a camera attached to your phone?" she asked. "How did you know that I have tattoos?"

I explained to her how my information is obtained; she seemed quite fascinated by it. Not wanting to lose my concentration, I continued on with the reading.

"Someone has a stolen traffic sign in a bedroom," I told her next.

"My son does," Jill screamed. "How did you know?"

"I not only know that, but my senses are telling me that you eat cookies instead of a meal, which is not nutritionally smart." I then heard something. "There is singing in my ears."

I waited for confirmation. At first, there was total silence on the phone. "You are correct in everything you have told me," she stuttered breathlessly. "I do eat cookies instead of a balanced dinner and I go to karaoke clubs all the time."

I asked Jill who Tara was in her family. She identified it as her sister's name

I revealed to Jill that I was now aware that Tara was confused and upset about her teenage son, Gregg, and had come to Jill for advice. Jill haltingly confessed to me that Tara suspected that Gregg was gay but was afraid to ask him.

So easy to read!

When Helene sat down at the fair, I thought of the song "Row, Row, Row Your Boat." She laughed and told me that she had just left a travel agency where she had booked a trip on a cruise ship.

"How was the rodeo?" I asked.

"Why, were you there too?" she answered.

"No, I wasn't there but I can see that you were there," I responded. Then, I heard taped music in my ear. "There is a DJ in the family."

"That's my son," she screamed loudly. "Were you at any of his parties? He's really quite good, you know."

I told her that there was never any type of encounter between her son and me, but I had been informed by my source that her son had a girlfriend who was a graphic designer. Upon hearing this revelation, Helene's mouth and eyes opened wide and she nodded her head "yes."

I asked Helene why I was hearing a *ding-dong* sound. She told me that her dog's name was Bell.

Messages all over the place!

Geraldine was dressed in a black, long-sleeved business suit. She did not look like the type of person who was involved in what I would consider extracurricular activities. The psychic message I received made me inquire about the 900 telephone number.

She sat there, obviously thinking about my question while looking quite surprised about it. Appearing flustered, she probably thought that I could not have known about this phone number. But since the reading had already started, she decided to be honest regarding it.

Geraldine told me that she had the number installed in her home so she could receive intimate phone calls from a private service. I informed her of the quiet whispers I heard in my ear. Her reply to this disclosure was that she talked about sex with her callers.

"There is a relationship between you and someone by the name of Neil," I then told her. Geraldine's eyes opened wide. She admitted that Neil was a steady customer.

Bulletin...my anonymous source knows all about it!

When Janine sat down in front of me at a psychic fair, my mind's eye saw two pairs of glasses. This indicated to me that she was being watched and followed—and that she knew it, as if she had eyes both on her face and on the back of her head.

She explained to me that she was being stalked by someone from her past with whom she had an on-and-off relationship. She had terminated her involvement with this man when she had discovered that he was engaged.

I guess he couldn't see what she could see was wrong!

Betty was a healthy-looking young woman. When she sat down for a reading, I immediately smelled the aroma of food. Upon relaying this information to her, she told me that she was a dietitian.

"Betty, you were asked to fire someone at your workplace," I said to her after being told this fact in my psychic hearing.

"Who told you that? Someone must have told you. It was the worst feeling that I could ever remember having," she replied.

"My source who tells me all the information is anonymous, and these communications aren't accessible to everyone," I answered.

Then, my senses were telling me that Betty was on a mission, searching for someone she knew quite well. When I told her this latest message I had received, Betty explained that she was looking for the man who had impregnated her and then abruptly left town prior to the baby's birth.

I cautioned her regarding the fact that his leaving was actually the best thing that could have happened to her. He was not a person of high character and wouldn't have treated her with respect, as demonstrated by his swift departure from her life. I finished by telling her that she shouldn't mourn his loss and it was fine that he was out of town and out of her reality.

Anonymous source, I keep telling them, but they don't want to listen!

Nikki came to the psychic fair and sat down exhibiting a manner of strong confidence. I was getting a message that she was quite an intelligent girl. This fact was indicated to me through a vision of many books in my mind's eye, and I told her so.

"Yes," she said and then added that she was a college student. Nikki was getting into the moment. "Please, tell me more," she begged.

A picture of mountains surrounding her came into my view and I told Nikki that this was a very relevant happening.

Her eyes opened wide and with a soft scream that scared everyone around us, she explained that a group of her friends had invited her to accompany them to a vacation lodge in the mountains. They subsequently had gotten into a car accident while traveling. They had been stranded...

My senses were then telling me about a serious relationship about which she had doubts, and I repeated to Nikki what was disclosed to me. She then admitted to me that she had recently broken off an engagement.

Where had I heard this before?

When Dora sat down in my house for a reading, my immediate psychic impression was that she was a very greedy woman. I informed her about the kidnapping plot that was on her mind. She verified my thoughts by saying in a very hushed voice that she was thinking of stealing her neighbor's cat. Her eyes were darting back and forth throughout the room even though we were the only two in the house. She seemed in obvious fear that her scheme would be discovered. Dora continued telling me about her plan, saying that she was sure that a large reward could and would be paid for the animal.

After telling Dora that it was not a smart way to make money, I suggested that she get a job instead of thinking of ideas such as that one. She told me she was sorry and realized how silly she must have sounded.

No need to talk quietly. There are no secrets here!

I watched Elijah walk towards me at a psychic fair. Even though he was dressed in a suit and tie, I knew that this was not his usual attire. I had a feeling that he worked outdoors, which required much more informal clothing.

Once we started the reading and I revealed this to him, he smiled and explained that he had worn a suit to try to test my ability to guess his occupation.

I asked Elijah who Mara was and this, too, impressed him because it was the name of his wife. I then inquired about the name Isaiah. He identified Isaiah as his father. My ability to give to him both his wife's and father's names seemed to leave him flabbergasted. He kept repeating it over and over. Then, he flattered me by saying that no other psychic had been able to do that for him.

Guess who was whispering it into my ear!

Rose was excited about her first reading with me. I was able to see cash, prizes and excitement around her. She said loudly that she had recently been a contestant on a game show and had won a car and a vacation.

I reported to her that my psychic senses were feeling the Caribbean Islands. Rose fervently screamed that the trip she had won had taken her there.

What lungs!

Anita and Mike came together for a reading. I had never met them before that day, so it was a pleasant challenge.

I told them that this was a second marriage for both of them and that they each had two sons who were twenty-two months apart in age. Anita did not even have to think about what I said because she knew that her sons were twenty-two months apart. She readily confirmed her part of what I had told them. Mike, after counting the age difference between his two sons, eventually agreed with this fact also.

Then, I enlightened them both with another piece of information that they hadn't realized: Anita and Mike were both also twenty-two months apart and had been born in the same hospital in Brooklyn, New York. Neither had realized these facts until I brought them to their attention.

My next statement was addressed to Anita and regarded the date on which she and Mike had been married. "I am sensing that you and Mike were married on your parents' anniversary."

She smiled, nodded her head and then told me that I was right. She explained to me that they had purposely chosen the date because her parents had a good marriage. Anita continued her story by telling me that both she and Mike thought that the date would bring them luck.

Then, I told Mike that he had experienced a problem with Anita's cat. Mike laughed and told me that he certainly did have a difficult time adjusting to living with an animal because he wasn't particularly fond of cats. But after living with Anita's cat, he could not picture life without her. He was now a cat lover.

I wonder how old the cat was. I should have asked. Never mind, I'll figure it out!

Helen called from upstate New York for her first telephone reading. I had never met her. Helen had heard about me from a friend of hers.

"I'm psychically hearing that you have a son named Peter," I began. "I'm also psychically seeing that he lives in Canada." There were a lot of messages coming through more than one of my senses.

Helen started to scream in disbelief. "Did my friend Millie tell you this?" she asked excitedly. "I usually can trust her with my secrets. I don't understand why she told you my business."

Calmly, I explained that the message "son, Peter" had been whispered in my ear. I also informed Helen that I knew about the Canadian connection when I saw in my mind's eye the vision of a stop sign written in French along with a view of many high mountains covered with snow. The reading was also showing me that I was definitely on the right track when a piece of cheese that said "Canadian" on the wrapper appeared shortly after the previous clues.

My next intuitive expression was a sensitive one, and I knew that it had to be handled discreetly. I relayed to her the feeling that Peter had originally gone to our neighboring country to avoid the draft during the late 1960s. In addition, my psychic vision was showing me that he had decided to stay there after meeting a young woman with whom he fell in love. Helen was again in shock that I was able to know this information.

She screamed, "I can't believe that you know about this. Are you sure that Mille didn't tell you? You have to tell me who told you."

I answered Helen just as I answer everyone else who asks me that question: "I just tell the truth. I do not know you or your family. This knowledge comes to me through the gift of clairvoyance. Thank you for the compliment."

It would be impossible to keep track of everyone's information. It's given to me new, fresh and straight from my anonymous source!

Rosie came back for a second reading. The first time I met her, she had been engaged to be married to a young man named Joe. I had bad feelings about this union and urged her to end her engagement.

On my advice, Rosie had investigated Joe's past and found many inconsistencies regarding what he had told her about himself. She thought about marrying this man and realized that it would be poor judgment on her part, and that she would eventually regret it.

She came back to me at the psychic fair to thank me for warning her in time. She said that she had nearly made the biggest mistake of her life.

One way or another, the truth would have eventually come out, but this certainly saved her a lot of time, energy and emotion.

Again, I want to give many thanks to my anonymous source!

Rhonda walked into the room looking for a psychic from whom she hadn't gotten a reading previously. She sat down with much anticipation and gave me a tremendous amount of energy to work with.

I informed her that I was hearing two names: Andrew and Justin. She told me that they were the names of her teenage sons. I felt that Andrew, her older son, had temperamental tendencies and was more of a challenge for her to deal with. He needed more direction than his younger brother, Justin, because Andrew was more intense, perceptive and sensitive. I also felt that he was loud, explosive, destructive and stubborn.

I relayed to Rhonda that Justin was more adaptable regarding his eating, sleeping and homework habits. My feeling was that he was dependable in his chores and errands as well as zestful, assertive and spirited in his life in general.

Rhonda asked me if I had ever hidden in her foyer closet. Of course she asked me this in jest, but it was her way of telling me how correct the descriptions of her sons' personalities were.

My answer to her was that there was never a need for me to hide in her or anyone else's foyer closet. In fact, I had never met her sons.

I'm positive that my anonymous source wasn't hiding in the foyer closet either!

Debbie was a young woman who I met at a psychic fair. She was looking for someone who could give her some advice about her future. I asked why she was having an identity crisis. Debbie became very excited, telling me that I had put into words the feelings that she had been having for the last few weeks.

I heard the sound of a band playing in my ear and told her about it, then asked for an explanation. Debbie told me that she was in a rock-and-roll girl group and had been thinking a lot lately about the ins and outs of fame.

I felt the name Vince around Debbie. She identified him as her manager. There were two other names I added to the list of people important to her: Madeleine and Joann. She told me that they were the names of two other singers in the band.

I told Debbie that I felt that Madeleine was going to leave the group with the goal of trying to make a career as a single act. Debbie told me that this fact was correct. Continuing the reading, I informed Debbie of my feeling that Madeleine did not want to share the stage with other performers.

With eyes open wide due to the accuracy of the reading, Debbie told me that Madeleine had informed Debbie and the rest of the band just the day before that she was leaving the group to try to make it on her own.

Good luck to Madeleine—a break from the pack!

Alan sat down for a reading and I immediately saw loads and loads of beds in my mind's eye. "Alan, you own a mattress store."

He agreed with the basic feeling of my reading but changed it slightly, saying that he didn't own a mattress store but managed a hotel that contained many beds.

Then, I told him about the many vehicles that I viewed. He told me that his father owned a parking lot.

"I'm also seeing many washing machines and dryers in my psychic vision," I added to this already lively reading. Alan told me that his mother owned a Laundromat.

I then threw the name Muriel out at him because it was loudly resounding in my psychic hearing. As soon as he heard the name, he appeared amazed—Muriel was his wife. Since I was on a roll, I also told him about the names Abby and Cindy, which I was hearing. They had to be important, and I was feeling that they were his children's names. Alan told me that these were the names of his twin daughters.

I had one other name to give to Alan, and I had no idea to whom it belonged. The name was Ralph. Alan told me that Ralph was his bird.

My next feeling concerned foreign travel. I relayed it to Alan. He answered that he was planning to go on a business trip to Europe shortly.

Alan then told me that psychic readings had never been of interest to him because he really didn't believe in them. But now he was a definite believer and would never make fun of the subject again. His curiosity about the paranormal had really given him an education not to be forgotten.

Being open-minded about a subject can actually open many windows for you!

John's reading at the fair started with my seeing racks and racks of clothing, so I commented to him that he had a large walk-in closet with a huge wardrobe. He expressed to me while laughing that he actually owned a dry-cleaning store.

I was hearing the name Margo and told John about it. He identified Margo as his wife. I continued the reading by telling him that I was feeling that there was some ongoing conflict within the marriage. The smile on his face disappeared and in a somber voice, he concurred. He explained to me that Margo liked to go out in the evening while he preferred staying home. Due to the fact that his store opened very early in the morning, he needed to go to bed at a reasonable hour in the evening. They fought about this subject continuously and he could see no end in sight.

I told John not to worry because there was a solution coming for him in regard to this stressful problem. He asked me what I meant by that. I happily informed him that Margo was several weeks pregnant and that shortly, she also would be too tired to go out in the evening.

John became very excited by this news and confessed to me that he and Margo had suspected that she was pregnant. Since it hadn't been confirmed by a doctor yet, he hadn't wanted to mention it to me. He told me that they had been trying to conceive a baby for several years with no success.

The happiness he was feeling came out in one of the broadest smiles I had ever seen. He thanked me for the good news and left on cloud nine.

He called me the following month and told me that Margo's pregnancy had been confirmed by a doctor and that she was experiencing typical pregnancy symptoms and was not in the mood to socialize in the evening. He ended the conversation by saying, "Thanks again!"

I didn't solve the problem, but thanks for the thanks anyway!

When Mickey sat down at the fair and told me his date of birth, which was under the sign of Aquarius, I told him that I felt music and auditions around him.

The name Adrienne popped into my mind and I was sure that it had to do with Mickey's reading. He acknowledged to me that she was the previous lead singer who had left his music group after being offered an audition for a television show. He answered, while smiling, that he held a job in a band that was currently holding tryouts for a new lead singer.

"Was the movie that you went to see all by yourself a good one?" I asked next. "And, by the way, I'm also being told that you were recently in a foreign country and got lost. I see you driving in a circle."

"Where are you getting this information from?" Mickey laughed heartily. "I did go the movies by myself and I was in Europe also, but what guy will admit to having gotten lost?"

My anonymous source knew where Mickey had been in Europe even if Mickey himself didn't know!

When Billy sat down for a reading, I told him to make sure that he had bandages because minor injuries were to be expected. He smiled and told me that he was involved with sports and usually suffered from multiple small injuries.

When I revealed to him my knowledge of his very intense feelings for someone by the name of Betsy, he smiled, saying that just the mention of her name made his heart pump faster.

Then, he said to me, "Did someone spike your water? You are right on target."

I don't need to have my water spiked. My uncommon psychic ability is something I was born with!

When Elliott sat down, he stood out in my mind's eye as someone who captivated crowds when traveling around the world. My first inclination regarding his occupational choice brought me to the conclusion that he was a magician.

But, it still did not satisfy my hunch. I needed to further meditate on what his skill entailed. Shortly after doing so, I realized that Elliott stood on a stage and hypnotized people. After I relayed these feelings to him, he smiled and confirmed his vocation. He told me that aside from doing hypnotherapy, he was also a behavioral psychologist.

I then mentioned to Elliott that I was receiving a psychic message that he was some type of hero. He was quite surprised that I knew he had rescued a dog from a burning building.

This guy was both intelligent and brave!

How Did You Know That? 153

Ross appeared to be a bit unusual and eccentric when I saw him at the fair. Although he wasn't wearing it, I psychically viewed an old arm cast and asked him what it was used for. He told me that he wore it so that he wouldn't have to participate in gym class. (The teacher just took his word for it?)

I saw a gravesite in my mind's eye and asked him who was buried in the grave that he had recently visited. He justified that vision by saying that he had just returned from visiting his grandmother's grave.

Then, I was seeing a comedy routine done on a stage. Ross informed me that his father was a stand-up comic.

Ross said that I was a psychic antenna. Birds better not sit on my head!

While on a cable television talk show, I received a phone call from Linda. She happily informed me that she was pregnant and the sonogram had shown that she was going to have a baby girl. The anticipated due date was during the month of February. She then asked me if I felt that everything would be alright.

I apprised her of the fact that she was going to give birth to a boy, not a girl, on December twenty-second. Several weeks later, she called to say that her son had been born two months early, on December twenty-second. Fortunately, everyone was well.

Certain things are just out of our hands—at least that's what I'm told by my anonymous source!

Stan had never been to a psychic fair before and was anxious to see if I was just trying to scam him. He warned me that he was very skeptical of my ways before he even heard anything that I had to say.

I told him that I felt a large portrait of an older woman around him. He answered that he had just purchased a frame for his grandmother's picture, which he was going to hang in the living room of his home.

I also described to him a psychic picture I was currently witnessing regarding his daughter, who was getting married. This vision was telling me that he was having a hard time adjusting to the fact that she would be leaving his home. He agreed and was totally shocked that I knew this. He promised me that he would never go to any other psychic because he was so impressed by what I knew about him.

Never say "never" about believing in something!

Sandy called me for a telephone reading. While she was talking to me, I began to visualize a house in an older neighborhood. I told her that I had a strong feeling that she wanted to go back in time and return to her roots. In other words, I asked, did she want to go back to live in her old neighborhood and perhaps buy the house in which she had grown up?

She told me—and probably everyone else in the neighborhood—with a loud scream that I was absolutely right.

But, I also felt that she wanted to add some visual appeal to her old homestead and had hired a designer to help make the old house more pleasant to look at.

Again, she screamed, "Who told you?"

By now, you must know who told me!

When Charlie sat down at the fair, my senses were telling me that he was in possession of a forged birth certificate. He became angry and said, "I want to know who informed you about this."

I told him, "My source is anonymous. My mind's eye is showing me an official document that has been tampered with."

He then told me that his daughter's birthday was one week short of the cutoff date for kindergarten, and since his daughter was quite smart, he called the governmental authorities and told them that he had lost her birth certificate. They had sent him a new one and he was able to change the year on it. He still had the original one for when she would need it later on in life.

Surprise—it's not a secret!

Francine called me on the telephone from Montana. She had gotten my name from her cousin, who lived in New York.

I immediately sensed that Francine had a deep tan, practically a glow to her skin, even though it was wintertime and she lived in snow country. It seemed logical to ask about her passion for tanning salons. When I inquired about it, Francine emitted a laughing scream. She asked me if there was a camera attached to my phone. After admitting to an addiction that had led her to join the local tanning salon as a lifetime member, she explained that she thought it made her look healthy.

Then, I perceived that she was having a trust issue with Ronald, her son-in-law, who was married to her daughter, Claire. Francine suspected that Ronald was having an extramarital affair. When I brought up the topic, Francine voiced her unproven fears to me. So, I meditated on the situation and realized that the belief was unfounded. My answer to her was that Ronald was just a flirt who called everyone "sweetie."

Don't look for troubles that aren't there!

Loretta called in to a radio show on which I was a guest and immediately my wrist began to hurt. I told her about it.

"Wow!" she replied, sounding shocked. She then explained that she was a victim of carpal tunnel syndrome. She was contemplating going to the doctor in the upcoming week.

When I heard the name Alexander whispered in my ear and then the sound of music being played, my next comment was in regard to the significance of this combination. Loretta told me that her son, Alexander, played the violin and that she was quite proud of him.

"Lenny is also your son, am I right?" I asked next.

"Lenny is my other son," she answered. "Tell me about him."

"Well, I can see that he has back problems," I replied.

"I am amazed that you know this," she yelled. "He not only has back problems, but he became a chiropractor because of it."

"Do your children have different fathers and is there a big age difference between the two boys?" I asked next.

"Yes," she answered, now laughing hysterically, "Alexander is eleven years old and Lenny is in his thirties."

Suddenly, I began to smell cooked food, so I mentioned to Loretta that my senses were telling me that cooking was something that was viewed quite seriously by Loretta. She sounded absolutely astounded. "I am planning to go to a culinary school to become a chef," she exclaimed, dropping the phone on the floor.

Loretta then told me that she was walking around the chair that she had been sitting on because she was too nervous to stay seated. She asked when she could call me to get a reading again. I told her to wait three months unless there was something serious she needed to discuss with me.

She finished our conversation by saying that she was totally enraptured concerning the whole psychic process.

Zach, are you listening?

Sandra called me on the telephone for a reading. I had never met her but knew when I heard her voice that she had been gardening recently near what she considered Fort Knox. When I revealed this feeling to her, she started to laugh and explained to me that whenever she did any gardening, even in front of her house, she locked the front door. I then added that my senses were saying that she even locked the door when she brought the garbage cans from the garage to the curb.

Knowing instinctively that Sandra had never been robbed, my next question was in regard to this unusual habit of locking the door when not necessary. She conveyed to me that she worried a lot about theft.

When I told Sandra of my feeling that she had been fired from her position as a registered nurse and was now a hairdresser, Sandra asked me who had informed me of this because it was all true. I explained to her that the knowledge came to me as I was shuffling the tarot cards, thus getting psychic messages, while she was speaking with me on the phone.

I will have to check it out to see if there is a garden in front of the real Fort Knox!

Jared had never experienced a tarot card reading and was semi-amused by it in the beginning. After a few minutes, he was shocked by his reading and quite honestly, I enjoyed watching his reaction.

I asked him if he had met his wife, Belinda, during his engagement party celebration. At that time, he had been engaged to someone by the name of Lorraine. Jared seemed astonished by my knowledge.

Continuing on, I told him that Belinda had been among the hired help at the restaurant where the celebration was held. Following this, I informed him that after the party he asked Belinda for her phone number, but she refused to give it to him because he was formally engaged to Lorraine. I then explained what my psychic senses were imparting to me: that he broke the engagement to Lorraine and promptly went back to the restaurant and asked Belinda for her phone number again. She gave it to him and, several months later, they were married.

I didn't ask, but I have the feeling that they skipped the engagement party!

Betty called me on the telephone. She told me that she had gotten my name and phone number from Lois, a steady client of mine.

As soon as she started to speak, I heard the number three in my head and asked her about it. She laughed and told me that she had three sons.

"I am seeing that you once used rope to tie one of your boys to the handle of the door leading to your garage. Is that true?"

"Yes, but let me explain," she continued. "I only did it once and I will never do it again. He was just so impossible that day and was teasing his brothers as well as chasing them. I was at my wits' end."

My next revelation totally startled her. I said, "You had surgery recently and the result was that you have a continually running nose while you eat."

There was total silence on the phone, and then Betty asked, "Who told you that? Did my friend Lois call you and tell you about that?"

"No, I am watching it in my psychic vision. And by the way, are the floors of your entire house, except for the kitchen and bathrooms, carpeted in yellow?"

Again, silence, followed by Betty screaming, "I don't believe it!"

"Alcohol played a significant part in the divorce from your first husband and you were set up to look guilty," I reported confidently.

"Yes, I am divorced, but what do you mean 'set up'?" she asked in a puzzled tone of voice.

"I'm feeling that your husband intentionally injured himself and then called the police, telling them that you threw something at him. He wanted you arrested. When the police arrived, they saw that he was drunk and you were asleep in bed. His story about you had no credibility."

"She had to have told you. There is no way you could have known this," she answered.

I didn't know it. It was told to me not by your friend Lois, but by…

Chapter Eight

Work, Play and More

A woman by the name of Pat came to me for a reading at a psychic party. She sat down and immediately I began to swallow incessantly. I could not stop. The smell of food permeated the air in my immediate area and I asked her why this was happening.

Pat told me that she owned a health food store and was curious about what the coming year would bring in regard to her business. Immediately, I saw in my mind's eye a man stealing money from the cash register. Pat explained to me that the only other person besides her who was permitted to work at the cash register was her manager, who was an old friend of the family. She then said that he was beyond reproach and that she would trust him with her life.

However, I continued to tell her that this "trustworthy" manager was not putting all the cash from the sales he made into the cash register. If any purchase was for an even amount of money and no change was required, he just put the cash in his pocket. But Pat was insistent in her judgment, repeating to me that this man was honest, sincere and genuine.

I gave her two suggestions. First, she should check the store's inventory against its receipts and perhaps even think about installing a hidden camera. Pat left my table wondering what to do, but was leaning towards taking my advice.

A week later, Pat called me on the phone and happily notified me of the truth of my reading. She had hired someone to install a hidden camera and upon reviewing the film actually saw the "honest" manager taking cash from customers and depositing it into his pocket instead of the register. Pat dismissed him from her employ. "I worked so hard to build up this business. Thank you for saving it," she said in an emotional outburst.

Don't swear for anyone—perception isn't always reality!

One Sunday afternoon, Jeff came to me at a psychic fair. I made an inquiry regarding the strong feeling I received that his occupation involved flying. Was he an airline pilot? He said that he wasn't.

He wasn't forthcoming with more information, but I still felt flying in the air. So, logically, I asked him if he owned a bird. He answered me in the negative.

Finally, he admitted that he recently became a certified skydiver. Perseverance on my part won out.

I just knew it. Nothing flies under the radar of my anonymous source!

Sharon, a petite woman with brown hair and a reserved demeanor, sat down for a reading. Immediately, I thought of the television character Howdy Doody, and I said so. She gave me a faint smile and remarked to me that Howdy Doody was what her son, Andrew, was called by his friends because of his red hair and freckles. She then conveyed to me the unhappiness the incessant teasing caused. It was all quite disturbing to her son as well as herself.

I was happy to tell her that her son's friends were going to be very surprised. When they saw the amount of success that was in store for Andrew within his chosen field, a new attitude would be initiated by everyone, including Andrew. I added that I felt that Andrew's selected area of expertise would be the entertainment industry.

Sharon, who could not hide her delight about my reading, proudly announced that her son was currently attending a performing arts school and was doing quite well. She was now beginning to smile.

I gladly added to her new cheerful attitude by saying that Andrew was talented and creative and was sure to be a major force in this field of his choosing. I told her that he was going to meet many new people who would be appreciative of all his abilities.

Time will tell us more than his friends will!

Rachel came to me for a private reading. As a former beauty queen, she possessed beautiful finger nails painted a bright-red color. After looking into her eyes, I thought of Humpty Dumpty. Trying to go over the entire nursery rhyme in my mind to see how it related to her, I realized that the phrase "tumbling down" was the key. Venturing my thoughts on the subject, I asked her if she had fallen down from a high place, such as a mountain or a roof.

Rachel howled with delight at my reading. She told me that her current job was to install and repair the roofs of commercial buildings.

Rachel seemed so feminine and delicate in her appearance and manner that I was surprised when she revealed that she was a roofer. The problem with her job was that she had fallen off a roof and suffered internal injuries, just like our friend in the nursery rhyme.

Who would have thought?

Mike sat down at my table for a reading and told me that he was a traditional father of three daughters…and that he was very involved with beauty pageants.

My first comment to him was that he only saw things in black or white, never gray. Mike laughed, nodded his head and told me that he was color blind.

The next reflection that I expressed to him was that although his children were not sickly, they were always at the doctor's. He then explained to me that his wife, the mother of his children, was a pediatrician.

I didn't feel that the children were attending school even though they were of school age. Mike affirmed my reading by telling me that the girls were being home schooled. They had been removed from their classes in order to prepare for their pageants and modeling jobs, and the school principal was not pleased. To make up for the educational loss, the family had opted to do home schooling.

An apple for the teacher? It doesn't matter what color it is!

When Artie came to the psychic party at someone's home, I asked him the identity of the woman spinning a hula hoop. He proudly explained to me that his wife, Toni, was a belly dancer.

After informing Artie that I saw mountains around him, he shook his head and laughingly told me that on weekends, he went mountain climbing.

My next vision, oddly enough, was of a cow, which prompted me to ask if he owned one. "Yes," he exclaimed in amazement. "I own many cows because I live on a farm."

That reading was different!

Connor sat down at a psychic fair and I immediately knew that someone in his close family had died when Connor was twelve years old. He nodded his head "yes," which told me that this was correct.

After explaining to me that his beloved grandmother had passed on when he was that age, he confessed to being traumatized by the loss. I began to feel that he had another major loss in his life at the age of nineteen and told him so; Connor disclosed that his other grandmother had died at that time.

I began to hear the name George in my psychic hearing, so I asked Connor who George was. He said that George was his boss at work. My psychic senses were telling me that Connor had experienced three different types of careers and none of them were related. Connor began to laugh, telling me that I was absolutely correct. Then, he enumerated them for me. The first was when he worked in a deli. The second one was as a truck driver and the third and current career was that of a landscaper.

This was a man who wanted to control his own destiny!

Danielle called for a phone reading. Since I had never met her, I had no idea what she looked like. My inner voice, however, was saying to me that she was a fashion diva.

After explaining to Danielle that I could see her painting, sketching, gluing and rearranging designs, she told me that her career was indeed fashion design.

I asked her who Christopher was. With what I'm certain was a big smile on her face, she told me that Chris was her husband whom she "absolutely adored." My mind's eye was showing me that he worked with his hands. Danielle said that he was an auto mechanic and a handyman on the weekends.

Here's another reading showing that we are all connected. Maybe he can fix my garage door!

Shane was a middle-aged man with a lovely smile who nervously sat down with me at a psychic fair. My senses were telling me that this was a man with numbers all around him. Upon giving him this revelation, he disclosed to me that he was an accountant.

Then, I felt that there were a lot of animals surrounding him as well. "Boy, you certainly have a lot of pets," I said in amazement. Shane laughed and explained that his wife worked at the zoo. Talk about bringing your work home with you!

While talking to Joanne during a telephone reading, I felt that she was involved with some type of a newscasting job. My inner voice was telling me that she was up to date on the latest information and breaking news seen on television. Joanne laughed and told me that the reason why she had opted for a telephone reading was because she knew that if I met her, I would recognize her and the mystique would be gone. She was, indeed, a news reporter.

I told Joanne that I was feeling that her mother's name was Doris and furthermore, I was being told that Joanne had a brother whose name was Kevin. I was hearing both these names and the relationships loudly in my psychic hearing. Joanne acknowledged my reading as correct so far.

My next thought was that Kevin had just started his own business and then hired his mother, Doris. When I voiced this latest message, Joanne told me that her brother had just opened a plastics factory and showroom and had asked their mother to be the receptionist.

Another feeling I was getting about Joanne was that her new assistant had to be watched carefully. I was sensing that he had the ambition to take over Joanne's position as a news reporter, and I told her so.

Even though it was the summer, my mind's eye was seeing mistletoe, so I asked her about it.

"Yes, it's true. I hang it in my house all year long," she answered haltingly.

"I'm also psychically seeing that you are writing a letter to Santa Claus even though Christmas isn't for another six months," I told her.

"Yes that's also true. I am actually writing it with my daughter," she said with a short laugh.

Then, some interesting feelings came to me regarding someone named Ted. I told her that Ted was a jealous and irresponsible man with a fierce temper. He was someone to be careful with regarding a personal relationship. Joanne told me that he was the man she was currently dating and that she was beginning to see these attributes in him.

I asked her what Ted's relationship was to bleach. She told me that during an argument she had with him, he, in an expression of rage, had poured bleach on her freshly dry-cleaned clothes.

It sounds like someone is going to be in need of an attorney. I'm not sure which one!

Rebecca was a petite, middle-aged lady who came to me for a tarot card reading. I told her that my psychic vision was showing me that she possessed a large amount of old furniture. She nodded her head "yes" and then told me that she owned an antique store containing furniture from past decades.

I told Rebecca of my feeling that she was a strong woman in excellent health but, for some reason, she would go into a hospital for an unnecessary surgery. Rebecca replied that she was in fine physical condition but was opting for cosmetic surgery, which was going to take place in a few days.

When I suggested to Rebecca that I felt a boat around her, she informed me that she had just returned from a cruise. She had an enjoyable time.

All you need to do is link everything together!

Terri began speaking with me at the psychic fair. She was a delightful young woman in her early twenties. In my mind's eye, I saw a gymnastic apparatus consisting of a horizontal bar suspended by two parallel ropes. When I described my vision to Terri, she proudly announced that she had quit her job as a secretary in order to work as a trapeze artist.

I was sensing legal problems around her. These feeling were confirmed when Terri revealed that she had just filed for bankruptcy.

My tarot cards were also showing me piles of mail. When I asked her what that meant, she brought to light the cards' reading that her boyfriend, Jeff, was working for the post office.

I was happy to tell her that I felt a lot of domestic happiness in the future for both of them. This, of course, was good news to Terri.

A bankrupt trapeze artist with a post office employee— and both of them content with life. They had each other and that was all that really counted!

When Bart sat down at the table for his reading, he didn't appear athletic but I felt that he was involved with sports. He told me that he was a basketball coach.

My mind's eye showed alcohol surrounding him. It was then that Bart disclosed that his wife, Candace, had a drinking problem but was working hard to overcome the addiction, difficult as it was.

I didn't feel that Bart or Candice smoked, yet there was a feeling that there were ashes in their living room. Bart told me that his mother had been cremated and her ashes were in a silver box in the family room.

Things aren't always the way they look!

Angie sat down at my table at the fair and I felt that artwork was part of her profession. She told me that she was an artist.

I also expressed to her my impression that there were children around her who were not her own. Angie explained that she was raising her widowed brother's children. When I asked her why I was getting a message about moving, she disclosed that she had mixed emotions regarding the fact that she would be getting remarried the following month. She was sending her nephews to live with her sister. Even though she was saying goodbye to them for a good reason, she was going to miss them.

Then, I saw two letter Ms in my psychic vision. She informed me that her two nephews' names were Mark and Matt.

Angie had been learning the art of being a mom!

When Liza sat down at the fair, I felt heart palpitations and told her so. She laughed and identified herself as a cardiologist. Then, I referred to Glenn, who was Liza's husband. She seemed shocked that I knew her husband's name.

When I expressed to Liza the feeling that her marriage with Glenn was one of convenience, without any deep convictions of love, she became teary-eyed and looked down at the floor. It was then that she asked me what the future held for her and Glenn.

My cards showed that the marriage was not a perfect match but with a little effort by both parties, they could eventually be good for each other. I felt that they were both psychologically damaged.

A football suddenly emerged in my mind's eye, causing me to ask Liza if she could relate to it. She blushed and then disclosed to me that Glenn was a former football player and was considered quite a catch by the ladies who were chasing him. They found out that they just couldn't hold on to him.

The doctor and the football player—interesting combination!

I received a phone call from Jeremy and immediately, I thought of a uniform and religion. Jeremy told me that he worked for the postal service.

He then informed me that lately, the location where he worked had been receiving dozens of letters addressed to "God in Heaven." There were no return addresses on the envelopes, so he didn't know what to do with the letters.

My anonymous source tells me that the messages are always received and they don't have to be written down!

I asked Jerry when he sat down at the psychic fair if he was striving to impress the new cashier by becoming the best worker in the store where he was employed. He admitted to me that he was trying to do just that.

Two nursery rhymes entered my mind. One was "there was an old woman who lived in a shoe" and the other was "one, two, buckle my shoe." I asked Jerry if he worked in a shoe store. He told me that he did.

It's not easy walking on water with shoes on!

Kay called me for a reading. She had gotten my number from a friend of hers.

I told her that there were courtroom trials around her. She confirmed my assessment, telling me that she was an attorney.

My sense of smell was indicating food, and I asked Kay what the relevance of that was to her. Kay divulged to me that she told any new acquaintances that she was a waitress.

I didn't understand why she would lie about her career choice, so I asked Kay why she would do that. Kay explained to me the fear she had regarding people asking her if they could borrow money if it was known that she had a successful career.

Then, I revealed to Kay that I could see an old car in my psychic vision, one that was much in need of repairs. Kay, using the same reasoning she had previously displayed, said that she purposely drove a very old car that made a lot of noise. She didn't want anyone to know that she was an attorney with a thriving law practice. She seemed to have some type of nervousness in this regard.

It had become a way of life for Kay to hide her achievements and she didn't seem to care if she had to make sacrifices to accomplish that. I assured her that success was nothing to be ashamed of and that she was foolish not to enjoy her life. She should have been honest regarding her occupation. A good start would have been to purchase a brand-new car.

I finished my thoughts on the subject by telling Kay that she shouldn't live life worrying about what other people thought. A person is only taken advantage of if he or she permits it to happen.

What is the benefit of working hard and having money if you're not going to enjoy it?

Kara was a middle-aged homemaker who came for a reading at a psychic fair. From her demeanor and the movement of her skirt, which was swishing and swaying with her every move, I didn't feel that Kara was being flirtatious, but was instead informing me about the bigger picture of her previously chosen career.

Kara explained that she was a retired professional dancer. I asked her who North was and she identified him as her former dance partner, Norman. North was his nickname.

My next comment was regarding my tarot cards, which were informing me that someone in her family was following the twelve-step recovery plan for addiction. She told me that her husband attended Alcoholics Anonymous meetings every week.

Addictions are carried by the entire family and show up very often in readings!

Troy sat down at the fair and I was feeling some mixed psychic signals. My instincts were telling me that his feet were agile and very powerful.

"You ride a motorcycle, don't you?" I asked. "It's parked next to a convertible in the garage. I can see it."

"Get outta town. Who told you that? You must know me and aren't saying," he answered.

"No, I've never met you, nor is there any previous connection with you, but my senses are also telling me that you have some extended family in Canada. In fact, you have a lot of family living there."

"Yes, I have family there," he mumbled while scratching his head.

"Well, getting back to your feet," I continued, "I'm being psychically told that they possess a great amount of power when used."

Troy explained to me that he was a professional ice skater and his hobby was riding motorcycles. He calmly told me that he had no fear of speed and in fact looked forward to getting onto the open highway and moving swiftly along, even without a destination.

Suddenly, I heard music around me. Troy told me that his wife, Beverly, was a songwriter.

She could write a song at any tempo for him!

Arnie looked like a confident and strong-willed person, but I knew that in reality, he was a very fragile being. He sat in front of me at the fair, sadly disclosing that he felt inferior compared to everyone he knew. He let others chastise him for things that were not in his control and was as critical of his own actions as others were of them.

As he sat there berating himself to me, I heard a voice whisper in my ear that Arnie would be offered a well-paying and rewarding job. Any debt he had could be paid, and this would initiate a new attitude towards life.

I repeated to Arnie the exact message that I was hearing, and he left the fair somewhat happy but still skeptical of the prophecy's outcome. He promised me that he would be back if the "dream reading" came true.

One month later, he returned to the psychic fair and sat down with a totally new outlook on life. He said, "Everything you told me turned out to be correct. Instead of me running after opportunity, good luck is chasing me. How can I ever thank you for your reading?"

My answer to him was, "You just did."

Arnie got what he apparently needed and deserved!

Nora, a forty-year-old woman, was born under the sign of Gemini, but I saw the sign of Taurus around her when she sat down at the fair. When I mentioned this fact to her, she told me that she had just purchased a Taurus model automobile.

When I asked her why I was seeing watercolors encircling her, she informed me that she was an artist who was working locally, trying to sell some paintings.

I also felt that Nora was stretching her muscles. Her explanation for that psychic feeling was the Pilates classes in which she was participating.

A picture of a camera suddenly popped into my mind. Nora told me that her husband was a photographer.

And, last but not least, why was there a picture in my mind of vitamins and minerals around her? She told me that her daughter managed a health food store.

The whole family got into that reading!

Jon looked much younger than his age and I found it startling. He told me his date of birth at the beginning of the reading and I was quite surprised when I learned that he was fifty years old. He appeared to be around thirty years old.

I sensed that he wasn't a womanizer, but my psychic vision was showing me that he chased girls. After I expressed this to him, he assured me that he was an actor and was currently playing the role of a womanizer.

Why was there also a feeling that he did a tremendous amount of exercise? Jon told me that he was currently making a fitness video in his spare time.

When I informed him that I was seeing a red heart in my mind's eye, he told me that his birthday was on Valentine's Day.

The birthday fit the role he was playing!

Roberto was a happy man who was anxious for his reading. I could hear music playing and was feeling publicity around him. I also saw traveling in my psychic vision and heard the word "surprise" in my psychic hearing.

He revealed to me that he was rock star and had planned a surprise visit to one of his devoted fans before leaving on a tour with his band.

How many fans would love a surprise visit from a celebrity!

Benny's first comment when he sat down at the fair was that it wasn't his first time there. He told me that he had gotten a reading from me in the past and happily, he was there to inform me that what I had seen and heard psychically had actually come to fruition. Even though he had strong doubts at that time that it would happen, things had started to fall in place for him.

I had previously suggested to Benny that he had a passion for jokes and laughter and desired a career devoted to both. In essence, he wanted to be a comedian.

Now, he had come back to say that his dream of being a stand-up comic had come to pass. He was now doing a routine in a comedy club and enjoying every minute of it.

My anonymous source thinks he's got quite a talent!

Susie had a musical career and I knew it immediately when she sat down for a reading because there was the sound of jazz in my psychic hearing and the collaboration of many talented artists in my mind's eye. Suzie agreed with the reading, telling me that I was absolutely correct. She said her career had been spread over a time period of forty years, which was, in reality, her whole adult life.

I revealed that I was hearing the name Joey very clearly. Susie told me that this was the name of her little grandson. Then, out came some important information that I was feeling regarding someone who was frightening Joey. I could sense that the bully was an older boy.

Susie told me that a teenager was trying to take over Joey's tree house. Her grandson was feeling very intimidated. The intimidation came through clearly in her reading, which showed how concerned she was for her grandson!

Don was a very loyal client of mine. He called me often and followed the psychic circuit. I could always be assured of his appearance at the fairs.

One day, when he approached my table at a fair, I sensed that he and his wife were going to become parents for the first time. When I disclosed this to him, he told me that my reading so far was correct. His wife had just seen a doctor that week and the doctor had confirmed a pregnancy.

"Are you thinking of changing careers? Whodunit?" I inquired.

"I sure am, Joy," he replied. He laughed and told me that once again, I was right. He was studying to be a detective.

We should team up!

After meeting Will and shaking his hand at a psychic fair, I told him that congratulations were in order for him. He thanked me and said that his wife had just given birth to a beautiful baby girl. Will told me that the feeling of being a father was something that couldn't be described.

I questioned him regarding buildings and drawings I was seeing. He disclosed to me that he was an architect.

A good career and the start of a new family is certainly something to be happy about!

Olivia sat down at a fair and I knew that she was in the medical field. My feeling was that she was a psychiatrist. She told me that she was.

I could see the color red, which very often indicates anger. Then, I asked her about the secrets that she had found within her daughter's private diary.

In a flustered manner, Olivia told me that she had read that her daughter, Cassie, was playing matchmaker for Cassie's father, Darren, to whom Olivia was still married.

I told her that Darren was actually enjoying this little game.

A psychiatrist is asking me what to do?

Adele came to me for a reading and my first thought was of an antique sewing machine. She informed me that she was a seamstress.

When I disclosed to her that my senses were showing me trains, Adele explained to me that her husband worked as a conductor for Long Island Rail Road. Unfortunately, he was not happy in this career.

The word *programs* was whispered in my ear, so I asked Adele what it meant. She told me that her husband was also a computer programmer. He had recently gone into this type of work as a second occupation.

Feeling that there were troubles in the marriage, I asked Adele about it. She confirmed this fact and told me that she had tried to restart the marriage by writing a book about her experiences with her spouse.

If only life could be so simple—if we could just program what we want and then receive it!

Tanya sat down at a psychic fair and immediately asked me if I thought she would go to hell when she died. I answered her question with my own question: why would she think such a thing?

Tanya then revealed to me that she did nude lap dances at bachelor parties. I explained to her that it was not for me to judge her when she could judge herself. If she was feeling guilty about her occupation, then maybe she should change what she did for a living.

I told Tanya of my feelings that she had been born on her parents' anniversary. She said that she was indeed born on her parents' special day and then told me that she and her parents celebrated their anniversary and her birthday together.

Then, I disclosed to her a psychic impression regarding a "money tree" received on her birthday. She laughed and repeated to me something that many of us have heard from our parents. When she was younger, she would ask for many gifts when the date of her birthday was approaching. Her parents would patiently make it known to her that "money doesn't grow on trees."

But, for her last birthday, they actually gave her a little tree with no leaves on it. Instead, it had rolled-up $10 bills on the limbs.

This was a girl who received money in unusual ways!

When Oscar came to me for his psychic reading at the fair, I saw a picture of engines, valves and cylinders around him. He told me that he built and repaired motorcycles for a living.

When I heard the name Ginger and repeated it to him, he identified that name as his wife's. Why was there a vision of faucets, pipes and sinks around her? Oscar smiled and told me that Ginger was a plumber.

Suddenly, I smelled pastries, cakes, soufflés and cookies. Was Ginger a woman who liked to bake? Oscar told me that she was constantly in the kitchen, making all kinds of confections for the family to consume.

No problem if the goodies fell down the drain!

When Melanie sat down for a reading I asked her if she wanted to check my vital signs. She laughed and said, "No problem." She then made it known to me that she worked in the medical field.

I also told her that I saw medical equipment. She identified her husband, Todd, as a technician who worked for a large medical group in a nearby town.

I was hearing the name Elizabeth loudly in my ear. Melanie quickly responded that Elizabeth was the name of her daughter. I was sensing physical fitness equipment around that name. She told me that her daughter was a certified personal trainer.

This is a family I wouldn't mind being stranded on an island with!

Sherry came for a first-time reading. I smelled flowers and saw shrubs and evergreens in my mind's eye. The pictures continued: corsages, centerpieces, basket arrangements as well as wedding and funeral arrangements.

You are correct—her husband was a florist!

From the time Joyce sat down for a reading, I could sense a creative style about her. I communicated to her the feeling that she was a teacher, but not a schoolteacher as most people know it to be.

Joyce smiled and told me that I was accurate in my assessment. She said that she taught women who were insecure about their bodies a way to embrace their natural beauty without extreme diets or cosmetic surgery. Joyce also advised her clients concerning clothes, undergarments and hairstyles.

I wonder what she thought about me!

As soon as Mitch sat down at the fair, I knew that he was adventurous. My mind's eye showed me that he was touring homes and specializing in global relocations.

He told me that this was actually so. He worked as a real estate agent traveling back and forth between California and Portugal.

His work certainly kept him going!

Hugh came for a reading on a Sunday, at a psychic fair. I could hear many conversations in my psychic hearing. When I suggested to Hugh that he was dressed for television but actually worked as a radio announcer and disc jockey, he told me that I was spot on.

I asked Hugh about his youngest daughter, Dawn, being very upset with him regarding a birthday. He said that he could relate to that and admitted that due to his busy schedule and preparation for the upcoming wedding of his oldest daughter, he had neglected a celebration of Dawn's eighteenth birthday.

Don't neglect one child's celebration for the celebration of another!

When Denise came to me for a reading, I communicated to her the feeling that she spent a lot of time traveling. I added to the reading that her husband had a drug habit that he was currently battling. I then heard loud music in my ears. This caused me to ask her if her husband was a rock star or in a band.

Denise told me that I was correct in all my theories. Her husband was a rock star, battling drugs and traveling throughout the country while performing in many large theaters. She told me that she went along with the band and was her husband's biggest fan.

It could have been a perfect life except for the drugs. If he only knew then what he knows now!

Pete called me on the telephone while he was flying as a passenger in an airplane. Unfortunately, he was in a different time zone and woke me up in the middle of the night. I felt badly for him because I knew that he was uncomfortable in an airplane. My sense was that a reading would calm him down.

I asked him if he enjoyed shopping because I had a feeling that he was always in stores. He told me that he was a buyer for a major department-store chain.

Maybe if he changed to a single-store job I could finish my night's sleep!

Luke was a fifty-year-old man whose chosen career was that of an actor. He had been professionally trained but was experiencing self-doubt and frustration and was very honest about it when he came to me for a reading at a fair.

Happily, I was able to report to him that he was on the verge of becoming a famous star in his area of expertise, which was of course, acting. The messages I received were saying that there was going to be a positive shift of fortune that would take away any negative feelings he had concerning his career.

I wish this kind of good message could be given to everyone!

I was happy to meet Scott for the first time at a fair. He was eager to speak with me and told me so. When I asked him who Patrick was, he answered that his father's name was Patrick. I had a strong feeling that I expressed to Scott regarding the fact that his father had a job that required him to work outdoors. Scott told me that his father was a construction worker.

My feelings were also telling me that Scott was desperately looking for some type of approval from his father regarding something that Scott was doing. I sensed that this good-looking young man sitting in front of me was holding back information from his dad, and it had to do with a career choice Scott had made for himself.

When I asked him about this message, Scott became visibly upset and told me that he feared disclosing to his father his current and future plans. He continued telling me that the occupation he had chosen for himself was not going to be masculine enough for Patrick. Scott then assured me that his father would think that it not only lacked masculinity but would say that it was downright feminine.

Scott had told his dad that he was a waiter, which was partially true. He was a waiter part-time. Scott's real job was being a ballet dancer.

I guess that Scott didn't have to worry about Patrick seeing him perform by accident!

Charlie was a physically large guy who came to my table at a fair showing pride in who he was. I knew immediately that he was involved in sports. He confirmed this message I was receiving by telling me that he was a professional athlete.

I told him of my feelings that he had a daughter named Lynn and when he confirmed this as correct, I immediately revealed that my senses were describing her as a young teenager who was a bit on the wild side. Charlie became pale when I told him this. It was as if I had opened up a floodgate of emotions he had not been able to discuss prior to our conversation.

He finally felt comfortable to speak about his daughter with a stranger. After candidly suggesting to me that she was more than a bit on the wild side, Charlie blurted out bitterly that she was completely out of control. He told me that at the tender age of thirteen, she had already had multiple sex partners.

My next revelation to Charlie was regarding a woman named Rose. He told me that Rose was his wife and the mother of Lynn. Charlie told me that Rose was quite concerned about the promiscuity of their daughter. He then informed me that the three of them were going to go for counseling, hoping that they could put an end to their daughter's way of life.

I asked Charlie who Paul was. Paul, he explained, was the name of the therapist who was going to be treating his daughter. They would be starting sessions that very week.

Another message from…oh, you know where it came from!

At a psychic fair, Wally sat down for a reading, I felt air and space. He confirmed this feeling by telling me that he was studying to become an astronaut.

Suddenly, I thought of Shakespeare's *Romeo and Juliet*. When I asked him what this meant to him, Wally laughed and told me that the girl he was dating was named Juliet but was called Julie by her friends and family.

After disclosing the fact that I was hearing a current popular singer performing loudly in my ear, he told me that she was his favorite musical artist.

Old culture and new culture!

When Fred sat down for a reading at a fair, I saw in my psychic vision a snowmobile crash on ice. Fred told me that his brother, Steve, had died in such an accident.

When I asked him who the policeman and the minister were, Fred replied that he was the policeman and his father was the minister.

Then, through my sense of smell came a delicious and savory food aroma that made me hungry. When I told this to Fred, he replied that his wife was a caterer.

Suddenly, I thought of Ebbets Field and the Brooklyn Dodgers. Fred smiled and sighed, telling me that he had been born in Brooklyn and had been a big fan of the Dodgers many years ago.

"What's up with the color green?" I asked after I saw the color in my mind's eye.

He laughed and said, "You're seeing the color green because my birthday is on St. Patrick's Day."

The information just kept coming and coming!

Jeff sat down at the table at the fair and I felt a lengthy renovation at a museum. I also was seeing an aircraft carrier that had been used in World War II and the Vietnam War, and for NASA recovery missions. After I verbalized this to Jeff, he told me that he had worked on the renovation of the Intrepid Sea, Air and Space Museum.

Then, I heard a symphony playing through my psychic hearing. Jeff explained this phenomenon by telling me that his wife was currently performing with a very famous orchestra. Her performance, he explained, included music from the greatest musical writers.

Two dedicated workers with different abilities!

I felt a catastrophe around Karen when she sat down to speak with me at a fair, and she confirmed this by saying that she had been in a near-fatal car accident.

When I asked her about the meaning of the mannequin I saw in my psychic vision, she verified my reading by saying that she owned a store that had mannequins in the window.

My next impression was of someone by the name of Roy. Karen identified Roy as her latest boyfriend. I was sensing that he was an actor who had just filmed his last episode of something for television. Karen appeared dumbfounded when she verified to me that the television show that Roy appeared in had just been cancelled.

Then, I began to feel hot water around Roy. Karen told me that Roy had been in legal trouble recently.

All kinds of information in this one!

Tina was a little apprehensive when we began her reading at a psychic fair but soon appeared very comfortable as I spoke to her.

I felt that this woman was quite talented. In my mind's eye was the picture of a dancer, and she confirmed that this was correct. After agreeing with this fact, she explained to me that she was currently studying privately with a former Broadway dancer on the upper west side of Manhattan. It was a musical theatre class.

I asked Tina if she was also involved in the art of arranging dances or ballets. She acknowledged this fact by telling me she was a choreographer.

After cautioning Tina that she was involved in too many things and needed to back off from so much stress, I explained to her that it would eventually bring her physical and emotional problems.

No matter how much you enjoy doing something, you need to know your limits.

When Harvey started to speak with me at a psychic fair, I became aware that he had an extroverted personality. I could also immediately sense young people nearby him in his chosen career. He identified himself as a school teacher. I knew that he had picked the correct profession because my impression was that he had the ability as well as the passion for giving that extra lift that young people often need.

When I asked him why I was being psychically told that he was going to make his mark on the social circuit, he told me that he was in a party mode and was seriously doing some networking to give his social life a little boost.

I assured him that he was moving in the right direction and not to worry because I had a hunch that he was going to meet the right people in the right places. There was luck all around him.

Sometimes, you can and have to make your own differentiation in this world. Go for it!

Lana sat down for a reading while holding a bottle of water in her hand. Immediately, I felt that soda was her preferred beverage and asked her about it. With a laugh, she told me that her husband owned a soda route and delivered the beverage daily to stores and residences throughout the local area.

Then, I said the word *firecracker* to her. She laughed again and said that her birthday was on the Fourth of July.

The next words that entered my mind were *strike a pose*. Lana agreed that it was an appropriate remark and told me that she was a model.

I asked her who Earl was. She identified Earl as her father and business manager.

At that moment, I got the feeling that Lana was going into a hospital for surgery. For some reason, I sensed that it wasn't a necessary surgery to correct a physical problem. After asking Lana why she was going into the hospital, she answered me that she was having some elective cosmetic surgery.

I thought she was beautiful just the way she was!

When Shelly walked toward me for a reading, I could see flames, but at the same time, I didn't feel that anyone around her was a firefighter. After expressing to her what my senses were imparting to me, she said, while laughing, that besides owning a candle shop, she possessed a large candle collection in her home.

I asked her who Jim was and she identified him as her boyfriend. I told her that Jim was packing boxes. Was he moving?

She told me that he wasn't moving but owned a moving company that offered packing and unpacking services for the customers who wanted it.

Who wouldn't want that? But I wouldn't want to pack by candlelight!

Marjorie looked no different from any other person who comes to me for a reading. But, I knew when I saw her that she was in a very difficult situation for many reasons yet to be expressed. I implied to Marjorie that her world went beyond the white picket fence and had traveled into deception and scandal. She asked me what I meant by that statement.

When I questioned her about someone around her by the name of Les, she disclosed that Les was her husband. I explained to her my awareness that her teenage daughter, Joan, was pregnant. Marjorie nodded her head and looked down at the floor, showing me that she was either ashamed or shocked that a stranger knew this fact. I went on to tell her of my knowledge that Les was serving in a very prestigious position in an educational institution. Marjorie again nodded her head "yes" and proceeded to tell me that he had just been elected president of this institution.

I knew that Les had been striving to show that he had a picture-perfect kind of family and was very embarrassed that his teenage daughter was now expecting a baby.

Marjorie, who worked five days a week, was agonizing over her daughter's pregnancy, blaming it on the fact that she wasn't home to supervise her daughter's friends and activities. She quickly acknowledged that money was not too plentiful and that she needed to work because the family's household expenses required a second paycheck.

I assured her that pregnancy in teenagers can also happen when mothers don't go to work. There are no guarantees in life about anything.

Marjorie was relieved to hear me say that. She said that I made her feel better, but now she had to figure out what to do about her baby having a baby.

The words *if only* are used so often in life!

Tricia came to a fair for a reading and when she sat down, I felt a confrontation between her and three of her employees concerning the workers' poor performances in the office. Tricia recollected the story easily, telling me that it had just happened the day before.

Then, I felt travel around her. She told me that she was the owner of a travel agency.

I also revealed to Tricia of my sense that there was a real estate professional dealing with her. Tricia informed me that she had just hired someone to find her a house because she was tired of paying rent.

I guess that Tricia would rather have stayed home and sent her staff traveling!

Mara had a very serious attitude when she sat down with me. I told her to stock up on lozenges because I was sensing that she was going to be verbally aggressive in the coming week. I suggested that her husband was going to feel her wrath.

She expressed to me that she had a lot of pent-up emotions regarding the fact that she wasn't in the financial position she wished to be in during that point of her life. Mara had become resentful and angry because of this turn of events.

My psychic senses were not revealing any major improvement in her financial status coming in the near future, so I assured Mara that she would not be able to depend on her husband to climb the corporate ladder as she wished him to.

I suggested that she get a job like the rest of us. Her husband wasn't going to be able to meet the demands that she was making of him.

Wishing doesn't always make it so!

A former contestant from a talent show contacted me for an appointment regarding his singing career. When I met with him, I apprised him of the fact that he would win three nominations for his acclaimed CD. I also assured him that he would receive offers from five major record companies.

The young man did win two award nominations and receive five offers from different record companies.

Can you beat that?

Ben met me at a psychic fair and I immediately felt like he had a yearning to be the white knight who would rescue a damsel in distress. He asked me what I meant by that. I revealed to him that my tarot cards were telling me that he liked to be the hero. He blushed and put his head down in embarrassment.

Then, I told him about the feeling of magic around him. He explained to me that his profession was that of an illusionist.

He did this as a full-time job. He then revealed to me his passion for being an entertainer.

I then informed him of my thoughts regarding a woman named Mary who was around him. I was feeling that she was quite frazzled regarding her children. He replied, with a laugh, that Mary was his twin sister, the mother of three toddlers.

Maybe he could make the children disappear until bedtime!

Chapter Nine

Sad to Say (But Sometimes With a Happy Ending)

A new client named Jeannie, who I met at a psychic fair, appeared to have a charmed life. Her husband, John, was very much in love with her and treated her with the utmost respect and admiration.

I felt a lot of moving around regarding her life, and she reinforced what I was saying by telling me that both she and John loved to travel; they did it quite often. In fact, they were world travelers.

Unfortunately, the knowledge of a negative life-altering change went through my mind as I reached across the table and felt her arm. Through this gesture, I was cognizant of the fact that John was suffering from advanced heart disease and that Jeannie needed to get him to visit a doctor quickly. Trying to be as protective as possible, I urged her to encourage John to get a medical checkup.

I didn't want to upset her, but it was clear to me that John did not have long to live. Knowing this, I again attempted to express my vision as discreetly as I could, considering the knowledge that was now possessed by me. I knew there was an urgency for him to get his financial affairs in order.

Jeannie followed my advice and encouraged John to visit his doctor. The physician acknowledged the heart problem and sent John to a cardiologist for more advanced treatment.

Six months later, John passed on, leaving Jeannie—who was mentally prepared to cope with her loss.

Life is never long enough for the people you love!

When Lois sat down with me for a private reading, I felt a power struggle and a battle of wills between her and her teenage daughter, Alison. It was almost like a cold war.

After establishing that fact, I asked Lois about the intimate pictures that Alison had taken of herself. Lois confided in me that she had just recently discovered photographs of her daughter that had been placed on the Internet for viewing by everyone.

In an attempt to make her daughter change her destructive ways, I suggested that Lois take Alison on a trip to see where this kind of behavior would lead.

Lois decided that she would take her to some type of detention center where wayward girls were sent. (Good luck to her if she could get Alison to go.)

The endless battles between mothers and daughters!

Janice sat down at my table for a reading and I immediately noticed her flawless skin. When I commented to her how attractive she was, she told me that she was a fashion model. After conversing with her for a short time, I realized that Janice was beautiful both physically and spiritually.

Unfortunately, my tarot cards and my psychic vision were telling me that she had a man around her who was an alcoholic, with many violent outbreaks of rage. Janice was in a difficult situation.

She admitted to me that her husband was very abusive, rendering brutal beatings to her quite often. When I inquired as to why she hadn't gotten an order of protection at the very least, Janice explained candidly that she loved him and didn't want to be alone.

Some women prefer to be abused rather than be by themselves. You can't make this stuff up!

Here is a similar story with a different ending.

When April sat down to speak with me, I knew she was a gentle person. Her demeanor made me think of a frightened bird.

Before she spoke a word, tears started forming in my eyes. I could sense that April wanted to speak but was afraid to. Even though there were no obvious bruises on her, I knew that she had been a victim of many beatings. I asked her who the six-foot man was in her life. That was when she identified the man I saw as her husband, Tim.

April then informed me that she was afraid to leave him because he had threatened to kill her and their children. This prompted me to advise her to seek an attorney for legal counsel.

Months later, April called me on the phone to say that she had ignored her husband's threat, moved out of the house and started a brand-new life that had to be better than the one she had.

It's frightening to hear some of these stories!

While on a radio show, I received a phone call from Fran who wanted to discuss her troubled marriage to Jim. In a hushed tone, so that her husband wouldn't hear, she divulged to me and the listening audience that she was hiding in a bedroom.

Upon shuffling my tarot cards, I commented that I saw her in my psychic vision, dressed in white and hiding in a coat closet. Fran confirmed both facts. She told me that she was a nurse and wore a white uniform. Fran said that every night when she returned home from work, she found her husband in a drunken state. He would beat her and then lock her in the foyer closet until morning.

Fran's children were grown and no longer lived at home. They were unaware of their father's recent behavior. The couple's extended family and friends were also ignorant of these facts. Jim's behavior in public was totally different from his actions during these drunken rages.

Although I usually don't encourage or promote divorce, in Fran's case, I advised her to see a lawyer. Months later, Fran called to tell me that she was dating a doctor. She sounded so happy.

Some people just need a little push!

Sad to Say (But Sometimes With a Happy Ending)

Barry called in to the radio talk show seeming very anxious to speak with me. I sensed that he didn't want to waste any time and that there was something weighing heavily on his mind. But, I could also sense a depth of character along with a code of ethics and was quite captivated by it.

I informed Barry that I was hearing bells and music that were involved with a tragic event. There was also a feeling perceived by me that Barry was unable to let go emotionally of an accident that had happened years earlier but seemed like yesterday in his heart.

Barry explained that while driving home from work one day, a six-year-old child ran out in front of his car. The boy was crossing the street after buying ice cream from a truck that had parked across from the child's house. The impact of Barry's car caused multiple injuries and killed the child immediately. That explained the music, the bells and the horrific event.

Barry tearfully disclosed to me that he blamed himself for the death of this young child. He also said that a part of him died that day. Although the child's parents forgave him, he could not forgive himself.

My first suggestion to Barry was to work on forgiving himself because this was an unfortunate accident. There was a destiny involved there that could not be changed. Then, I advised Barry to move away from the area in which he lived, since this depressing happening occurred in his own neighborhood. In this way, he wouldn't have a constant reminder of that day's events.

I recently spoke with Barry and he admitted to me that he is slowly starting to function without sorrow negating everything positive that he does. I comforted him by saying that he will never forget that afternoon, but it will eventually not be on his mind every minute of every day.

Time might not heal completely, but it does heal somewhat!

I met Fred while I was working at a psychic fair. My senses told me that he was in turmoil. He seemed very agitated. After peering with my psychic vision into his history, I was able to ascertain that he had been in a car accident recently. Sitting before me was a traumatized person.

My tarot cards were also telling me that he worked with computers and was content with this occupation due to the fact that it fulfilled his monetary needs. His life had seemed to be on track until the accident occurred.

Fred answered in the affirmative on both issues. He had been stricken with a brain aneurysm while driving and as a result was involved in a car accident, and had to leave his job in order to recuperate. The incident forced him to move in with his mom and apply for disability. This was upsetting enough, but not as bad as the breakup with his girlfriend, Lydia. Lydia had been his significant other for many years but had decided that she could not deal with this new issue.

Fred was depressed and nervous. I felt that he had bruises on his body although they were not visible because he was wearing a suit. He admitted having them and told me that the physical scars hadn't been caused by the car accident. He relayed the cruelty that his siblings had inflicted upon him. This included physical beatings and verbal teasing due to the fact that he had to move back with his mom.

All of the above-mentioned events and circumstances made Fred feel that he had nothing to offer anyone. I tried to encourage him to start a new life and try to forget about what had recently happened. For this reason, he became a steady client of mine and a sincere and genuine friend.

The last reading that I gave him showed me that he was about to suffer another aneurysm. I needed to warn him because it was important that he be prepared, which meant that he shouldn't be driving again. I feared for his safety as well as any innocent people who might be unavoidably hurt.

My psychic vision informed me that he would arrive home without incident, since it was a short distance from where we sat, but I didn't want him to drive after that. After describing this last visual, I also told him to make a doctor's appointment for the next day to have the appropriate tests which would determine if there was another brain aneurysm developing.

Fred assured me that he was able to drive and promised to call me when he returned home, which he did. Even though I had advised him to go to the doctor the next day, I knew that this was going to be our last conversation, and I was feeling great sadness about it.

The following morning, his mother called me on the telephone to say that he had suffered another aneurysm in his sleep. She had found him in his bed that morning.

I think of Fred often and realize that there is some truth to the saying "the good die young"!

One evening, while I was working on a talk-radio show, a gentleman by the name of Jeff telephoned in for a reading. I went into meditation mode and was able to zoom in on an interesting story.

My psychic vision was telling me that Jeff wore a job uniform and was on duty through various shifts. He confirmed my reading by admitting to me that he was a police officer with a varied schedule. I conveyed to him my feeling that he was working too many days and that his work schedule was going to take a toll on his health. It was then that Jeff told me that he worked at another job on his days off.

I asked Jeff if he had experienced a loss recently. He expressed how sad he was that his wife Audrey had suffered a miscarriage.

I didn't want to tell him that my intuitive senses were saying to me that Audrey had opted to abort the baby because she was unsure of who the baby's father was. I was also receiving information about her fear of gaining weight. It would have been a difficult issue for Jeff to understand at that particular moment. Sometimes, things are better left unsaid.

Meanwhile, Jeff continued telling me how disappointed he felt regarding the couple's recent loss, which led me to suggest that he quit his second job. Maybe he needed to spend more time with Audrey. I carefully asked him if he thought there were some degree of deception occurring in regard to his wife. Jeff wasn't really surprised by this question. He informed me that he and Audrey had just renewed their wedding vows because of his recent discovery that she had been unfaithful to him.

Sad to Say (But Sometimes With a Happy Ending)

I advised him that his marriage had many obstacles to overcome and suggested that they go for counseling. Healing is very difficult to achieve, but if there is some degree of love and a sincere attempt, it can happen.

You fell in love to begin with!

I met Justin at a psychic fair. As soon as he settled himself across from me, I saw balloons and flowers is my mind's eye. When I told him this, he semi-happily announced to me that he had just given his wife balloons and flowers on the occasion of the birth of their first child, a son.

Strangely, he did not appear to be too excited about the event. When I questioned him about it, he admitted that he was feeling depressed. It was then that a feeling of deception came over me. I began to feel electrical impulses in my fingertips. This sensory perception told me that Justin had visited a psychic during his wife's pregnancy and had been told that he was not the biological father of the baby. Justin told me that my reading so far was correct.

I then happily informed him that the other psychic had been wrong. This was his biological child. He suggested to me that I was just being supportive, but I assured him that no well-meaning psychic or clairvoyant would ever purposely give an inaccurate reading or lie to a client. This baby was definitely his.

A month later, Justin came to see me again and told me that he had been considering having the baby's blood tested to see who was correct—me or the psychic he had visited previously. (Remember Tammy's story?) But, he had decided not to because his son looked exactly as he did when he was a baby. In fact, Justin brought a picture of himself as an infant and a picture of his new offspring. The photos looked so alike that any observant person would say that they looked like twins.

It's amazing how much trouble can be started by someone who doesn't know what he is doing or saying!

Laura attended a psychic fair with her husband, William. As soon as she was seated, I smelled coffee brewing in a coffee maker. However, the faster the coffee was brewing, the more I could sense that this woman had violence around her.

Upon informing Laura about what my senses were revealing, she admitted to me that her parents had subjected her to extreme physical abuse. She explained that because of her depressing upbringing, a normal life seemed far removed from her reality.

Because Laura felt that she could not confront her parents in regard to their treatment of her, and therefore close a painful chapter in her life, I recommended that she seek professional help. (I have heard so many stories similar to this one.)

While we were speaking with each other, William sat down at a nearby table for a reading with another tarot card reader. Laura glanced at him and asked me if I was attracted to him. I answered that I felt no attraction towards him. Suddenly, Laura stood up and screamed, "He's not good enough for you?"

Unfortunately, the police had to be summoned, and she was escorted out of the building. It was, I'm sure, very embarrassing for Laura...or maybe not.

Counseling, anybody?

Leah sat down for a reading at a psychic fair appearing very distraught and distracted. Immediately, I felt a teenage girl around her and heard the name Melanie. When I mentioned this name to Leah, she informed me it was the name of her daughter.

I focused my psychic energy on Leah's eyes and saw that Melanie was being bullied and tormented at school on a daily basis. Leah explained that Melanie did not want to go to school but would not tell Leah why. Each day her daughter had another excuse to skip classes. Now Leah knew why.

A week later, Leah called me on the phone and advised me that Melanie finally admitted the reason, confirming what I had seen in my reading. Mom and daughter spoke to the school guidance counselor and the situation was resolved.

A common situation with an uncommon ending!

A client by the name of Rhonda called me. She lived in Manhattan and had been referred to me by a friend of hers.

As soon as she began to speak, I saw in my mind's eye a big building containing many pieces of fine art. Rhonda disclosed to me that she worked in a very famous museum in Manhattan. I was able to name her place of employment, which was very exciting to her. Rhonda admitted to me that she was now a believer in psychic phenomenon.

My next auditory revelation concerned someone by the name of Lawrence. She told me that her father's name was Lawrence, and her husband's name was also Lawrence. In addition to that, she had a nephew who was called Larry.

Rhonda then informed me that she was planning a trip to the Caribbean Islands in the fall. She wanted to know if she would enjoy this vacation. After meditating briefly on the issue, I apprised her of the fact that the trip would be suddenly cancelled.

After the summer had ended, Rhonda called to tell me that the trip had indeed been called off because her husband had become seriously ill. I was truly sorry to hear about Lawrence's illness and was even unhappier that my psychic senses were telling me that his health wasn't going to improve.

It's as difficult for me to know the reality as it is for the recipient to hear the truth!

When I first met Ben at a psychic fair, I smelled the beautiful fragrance of flowers. When I inquired about it, Ben told me that he owned a florist shop. In my mind's eye, I saw him traveling back and forth. He conveyed to me that he had a long-distance romance with a married woman on the West Coast. However, due to her marital situation, she had decided to finally end the affair with Ben.

This was where the interesting part ended and the scary part began. Ben, who had become a fan of mine, suddenly became a stalker. He asked me to light a magic candle and perhaps perform some type of miracle in regard to his ex-girlfriend. He wanted me to place a black cloud over her husband. I explained to him that I did not have that type of power and wouldn't put a black cloud over anyone, even if I could. I advised him that I don't make things happen, I just report them. He continued to harass me and ultimately forced me to file a police report that led to an order of protection.

Fortunately, Ben's requests could not be performed by a mortal. It just seems that way!

Sam called me for a psychic reading. I immediately felt that he was struggling economically while trying to lift himself out of poverty. Sam confirmed my vision by telling me that his only income was from Social Security.

Then, the word *century* came into my mind. I asked him if he could relate to that, and he told me that he was planning a birthday party for his mother, who was turning 100 years old the following month. He was her sole caregiver and wanted her to have a small party. It was not going to be elaborate, but it was something that he knew she would appreciate.

Then, after seeing the color red in my mind's eye, I inquired if he had recently purchased something in that color. He laughed loudly and then said that he had just bought a used red car with a lot of mileage, but it was the only automobile that he could afford.

When I began to see the initial W come into my psychic vision, I knew it represented a female around him. I could also perceive that she was disabled.

Sam informed me that his daughter, Wanda, was handicapped. She had been born with a birth defect.

Think about this story the next time you feel sorry for yourself!

When I saw Victoria walking towards me at a fair, I thought of the kind of girl every mother would want her son to marry. Knowing that this girl had lost a tremendous amount of weight, I revealed to her what my vision was telling me. She confided in me that she had lost, as she put it, "an amazing amount of pounds."

When I mentioned that there had been a mishap around her and that she had recently started a new job, her mood changed to sadness. She then made it known to me that her young daughter had passed away and that she had channeled the grief into a new career.

Life is always changing, and a new career can sometimes help heal some of the pain!

Jay was a successful, middle-aged man who had come to a psychic fair for a first-time reading. I was sensing that a lazy and unmotivated adult child was living with him. He assured me that the beginning of this reading was totally correct. He felt that his son, Kirk, who was twenty-five years of age, had long since overstayed his welcome and needed to find employment so that he could get out of Jay's house and become independent.

I told Jay that my psychic hearing was telling me that Kirk had accrued $100,000 in debt, and that Jay had paid it. Jay confirmed the amount as true.

Sounds like Jay created his own problem!

When Ron sat down for a reading, my tarot cards were informing me that he was a construction worker, a fact that he unhappily confirmed. He quickly added that he hated his current job. Ron said that he was feeling "trapped."

I was sensing the letter C regarding a woman who was very close to him, possibly his wife. Again, he confirmed what I was saying by identifying the letter as belonging to his wife, Carla.

Then, I felt animals that were coming and going. I asked Ron if he and Carla were foster parents to pets. He explained to me that he and Carla had a problem making commitments to any animals, so they rented pets. He assured me that it was the new trend.

I truly didn't want to hurt Ron, but I explained to him that having a pet was not a novelty. It was a long-term commitment. Pets bond with their owners and it is cruel to force the animals to break ties with their guardians. Our furry friends are very sensitive and connect with those who are their caretakers. I was honest with him and expressed the feeling that he was being unfair to the animals by sending them back to where they came from.

Ron said that he couldn't become emotionally attached, but he did not know that animals bond with those they live with.

Maybe he should have bought stuffed animals. Then no one would suffer!

Clara came to me for a reading just for entertainment purposes. She told me that she was a mother of four and appeared to be grateful for a devoted and faithful husband named George.

I asked Clara who April was. I knew that my reference was not talking about the month, but about a woman with that name around her husband George. I was also seeing in my mind's eye three letters: V, G and I.

After pondering all that I said and visualized, Clara confessed that she had no idea to whom or what I was referring.

Continuing on, I expressed my awareness that George traveled a great deal of the time. Clara confirmed my psychic feeling by telling me that he was away for weeks at a time. I reached for Clara's hand and told her that George was leading a double life. I perceived that her husband was devious and deceptive. She left my table very confused.

Months went by and Clara came to me again at a psychic fair for another reading. She told me that George had passed on and present at the funeral was a woman by the name of April. Clara didn't know who this woman was but then realized that

Sad to Say (But Sometimes With a Happy Ending)

I had been correct after all. April admitted to being the other woman in George's life.

When Clara returned George's leased car, she looked at the license plate and realized that the three letters that I had given to her in the reading matched the first three letters on the plate—VGI. She had previously thought that the letters stood for "very good intentions." Now she knew that George was leading a double life and that it was not by accident—it was intentional.

George's only intention was taking good care of number one!

When Lilly sat down at the psychic fair, I felt total depression emanating from her. She told me that she was very upset regarding her financial situation.

I was happy to tell her that there were going to be surprise events and circumstances thrust upon her. Lilly seemed very confused. I mentioned to her that she was going to inherit a large amount of money, which would put an end to the financial problem issues that were plaguing her. Then, I told her that she was going to participate in an unexpected event that would ultimately bring her romance, love and happiness. I was sure that the man she was going to meet would own a boat.

Lilly laughed at my prediction and assured me that she didn't go out often because she was in chronic pain from a car accident that had occurred many years earlier. I continued my reading by telling her that I felt that there was some type of remedy on the way. With all this in mind, I suggested that she attend a party at a country club to which she was going to be invited.

The following month, Lilly came to a psychic fair to see me again for a new reading. Her cheerful mood and happiness must have been conveyed to all who saw her. She couldn't stop smiling.

She confirmed to me that each of my predictions for her had come true. First, a distant relative had passed away, leaving Lilly a large inheritance. Then, she had met the man of her dreams at an event at a country club. This new man in her life not only owned a boat—he also owned a yacht club.

Lilly was so appreciative of my previous reading, but she didn't realize that I didn't make this good fortune happen.

I just heard about it from you know who.

Helene was an elderly woman who came to a fair for a reading and was very enjoyable to speak with. She had a quick wit and a sweet disposition, which made the reading even more pleasurable to do.

My question to Helene concerned someone by the name of Susan. I asked Helene who Susan was and why there was something that was bothering Helene concerning Susan's welfare. I was feeling a car involvement.

"Oh, she is my little granddaughter who I am very concerned about," she answered.

My next question was in regard to someone by the name of Camille. Helene told me that Camille was her daughter-in-law and Susan's mother.

"What was the concern regarding Susan's welfare?" I inquired.

Helene looked around to make sure no one was listening and then confided in me that Camille was leaving Susan in the car by herself whenever errands needed to be done, whether it was to the pharmacy, a bagel store, the dry cleaners' or the donut shop.

I assured Helene that she had every right to be concerned. She should tell her daughter-in-law that leaving a child so young in the car was against the law. My anonymous source was apparently giving a message through me, forewarning the family that this was a dangerous pattern of behavior in regard to Susan's safety.

Warnings are given for a reason. Heed them!

I had never met Ned before he came to see me at a psychic fair. I asked him if his uncle was also his stepfather. Ned seemed shocked that I was able to know this. He explained, in an extremely low voice, seeming fearful that anyone else would hear him, that after his father died, his mother married her husband's brother.

The feeling I was having indicated to me that Ned was having a hard time adjusting to his mother's marriage. Ned agreed, saying that he was indeed struggling with the situation.

I saw in my psychic vision that Ned was divorced but also a determined father who was trying to gain custody of his son. The name Roger was whispered in my ear, so of course I asked him who Roger was. He received this question with a look of disbelief. He confirmed to me that "Roger" was the name of his son, his only child.

Ned then told me that the custody fight was very bitter and that Roger, who was a sensitive youngster, became upset easily about the continuous fighting.

Every male in this family had a story!

Maura, a teenager, called and asked for a telephone reading. I happily obliged her. She had gotten my number from her friend's mother.

The first message I received told me that she was skipping many days of school. She answered that this was indeed correct.

"What's with the prank telephone calls?" I asked.

"I have fun doing that," she replied.

"But many people have caller ID. Aren't you afraid that you will get caught? This is not acceptable behavior even if people don't have caller ID," I continued. "You will be in serious trouble. I don't even have to be psychic to know that."

There was total silence on the phone line. She was eager to move on and was not going to be dissuaded from doing things she considered fun.

After sensing the feeling of body needles, my next question was whether she had body piercing done to herself. She answered again in the affirmative.

I knew that Maura was being blackmailed by an unethical photographer. Maura confirmed this fact and told me that one day she had seen improper pictures of herself on the Internet.

She was definitely a rebellious teenager whose pictures didn't get on the computer by themselves.

After asking her if her parents were going to send her to live with her strict grandfather, she replied with a choking voice, mumbling a sad "yes." Maura told me that all my visions were true.

Always think about the possible consequences of your actions!

Barney was a man whose fine character was evident to me from the time he sat down for a reading till the time he left my table.

I knew that he was battling a life-threatening disease. He verified my feeling, saying that he had cancer, and then told me that although he found it a difficult disease to fight, he was determined to challenge it by keeping himself in a positive frame of mind.

I asked Barney if he had twins in his family. Before I even had the chance to tell him their names, Barney proudly announced to me that their names were Selena and Samantha.

His courage will show his daughters strength of character and fortitude!

Ann was a teenager whose sadness appeared in an aura around her. She was sitting in front of me for a first-time reading with a sad face, looking as though she would burst into tears at any moment.

I asked her if her father had passed away suddenly, leaving Ann heartbroken from the loss. She looked at me in a totally surprised way and asked me if I were a mind reader. I explained to her my ability to sense her psychic energy and in regard to her, the vibes I received were of hopelessness and despondence.

I told Ann that her father had been her rock and that she felt fearful of going out into the world without his presence and guidance. High school graduation would be taking place soon and I knew that she felt as though her best friend and entire support system was gone.

I assured her that life is something precious and relatively short. Someday, she would see him again. In the interim, he was watching over her from another dimension and would be very proud of her if she honored his memory by being everything he wanted her to be.

Our loved ones are just a thought away!

Rod was anxious to talk to me about his problem when he sat down at a fair. I told him that he had a child, but not his own biological child.

Rod confirmed what I said. He told me that Joey was his new stepson and that both of them were having problems adjusting to their new roles. Joey was not accustomed to having a male around both him and his mother. He was also still loyal to his biological father, a little jealous of Rod and protective of his mother. This was hurting the mother's relationship with Rod. The situation brought a tremendous amount of tension into both of their lives.

Sad to Say (But Sometimes With a Happy Ending) 219

I assured Rod that eventually Joey would adjust to his new family and if not, he would eventually grow up and then understand the dynamics of having a new man in the house.

Many problems, even though they might seem like they will, don't last forever!

When I asked Brian why his dream girl, Molly, had turned against him, he explained to me that she had been mistakenly led to believe that Brian had a criminal record. This young man sitting in front of me at the psychic fair looked absolutely distraught.

He continued his story by telling me that he did not know how to undo the damage that this falsehood had created. Molly refused to see him or take his phone calls. He had been trying to contact her for weeks.

Whoever told Molly this falsehood will possibly have a lie told about him or her. Let's see how that person likes it!

When Roy walked over for a reading, my first impulse was to ask him who Fran was, so I did. He told me that Fran was his wife. Then, I asked him why he was destroying his children's spirits by cursing them and hitting them. I was also sensing that he did not care to participate with childcare or help with the housework.

Roy protested my reading by saying that everything I told him was correct, but he wanted to justify why I was feeling that way. He attempted to clarify his position by telling me that he didn't think that he was abusive to his children because kids needed to be disciplined. He also reasoned that his role as the family moneymaker was purposeful enough, meaning that he didn't have to help with the duties of cleaning and cooking.

I explained to him that he was hurting his children with his domineering attitude and that he needed to take more of a role in the family unit. Being the one who brought home the paycheck was not the only position that he should have held within the family.

Several weeks later, Roy came back to the fair and enthusiastically reported to me that he was contributing more than his weekly pay to his wife and children and he was honestly finding it more rewarding.

Never too late to learn from your mistakes!

Joe seemed to be very serious when he sat down with me for a reading. I began to feel that there was an estrangement between him and his relatives. He admitted to me that he wanted to go back to his family, with whom he no longer had any contact.

I asked him what the writing was about and he told me that he was a journalist. This was his way of expressing his creative talents.

Then, suddenly, my psychic hearing was giving me a message of piano music. When I questioned Joe concerning this message, he told me, with a wistful sigh, that his twelve-year-old brother was able to deal with their mother's schizophrenia by playing the piano.

People deal with problems in so many different ways!

Charlotte was obviously upset when she sat down for her reading at the psychic fair. I told her that I was hearing the name Buddy and was being told that there was a fight ensuing over him. Looking sadly into my eyes, Charlotte explained to me that Buddy was the name of a ten-year-old dog that had become the object of a struggle over ownership.

She continued her story, telling me that her oldest daughter, Marie, would be moving out of the house and getting married shortly. Several days earlier, Marie had announced to the family that since Buddy had been bought originally for her when she was younger, it was only fair that Buddy come and live with her.

I asked Charlotte who Holly was. Charlotte said, in a low voice filled with emotion, that Holly was her younger daughter who would be distraught if the dog were removed from the home by her sister.

How can I ask someone to get a new dog?

I knew that Elena was an intelligent woman after meeting her at the fair, but I could psychically see that she was frightened and nervous regarding her parenting skills. Upon my telling her this, she expressed to me her fears regarding her adequacy in raising her son, Scott. He was currently in nursery school and experiencing problems with it.

"I am hearing the name Gladys," I told her. "Can you relate to that?"

"Gladys is my mother," she replied with a surprised look.

"Why aren't you reaching out to your mother or Scott's teacher for help and guidance?" I asked next. "Don't you think that they could be of some assistance?"

She explained to me that her mom was very proud of her and asking her mom for help would indicate that Elena was a weak person. She continued by saying that her mother would also not be pleased if the teacher were made aware of the problems because the teacher was an outsider.

Always be truthful about your weaknesses. Admitting weakness indicates strength!

Meredith was very quiet when she sat down for a reading, but I knew that she was in deep distress regarding a divorce that had happened within her family. When I repeated the information that I was receiving, she admitted that her parents were divorced and that her father was dating someone just a few years older than Meredith.

When I asked her about the tension and worry regarding money, she brought to light the fact that there was no available cash because her father had emptied all of the bank accounts before leaving her mother.

What a nice guy!

Sad to Say (But Sometimes With a Happy Ending)

Diana and Mel, a lovely married couple, came to me at a fair for a reading. They told me that they had just adopted a baby girl who they thought was just adorable.

Unfortunately, I sensed blood and legal issues around them. Mel told me that I was correct. He had just gotten a message from his attorney that the birth mother wanted her daughter back.

I knew that I had to prepare these people for the inevitable task of returning their adopted daughter to the woman who originally gave her up. This was not going to be an easy thing to do.

I explained to them that it was perhaps not their destiny to raise their newly adopted child during this lifetime. Unfortunately, this was a situation that was out of their hands.

I give the answers from the messages that I get. My anonymous source knows the whole story!

Justin explained to me that he felt like an awkward teenager who epitomized the way adults saw kids of that age group. He was sitting across a table from me and appeared to be furious with all adults.

I inquired about a man named Nathan around him who was a writer. Justin admitted to me, with very little enthusiasm, that his father, Nathan, was an author who had recently written a book concerning the supernatural. His dad had gotten the idea for this fictional endeavor from the house that the family was living in—he suspected that it was haunted.

When I told Justin that I was psychically hearing about the everyday struggles between him and his father, he acknowledged that he and his dad fought about everything and agreed upon nothing.

The feeling of awkwardness felt by a teenager is compounded when there is no respect for his or her views!

When Margie sat down for a reading, I told her I heard the name Johnny, who was identified as her son. She confirmed this as the truth but seemed stunned that I knew this piece of information.

I saw in my psychic vision an accident that involved a small boating vehicle resembling a motorcycle. When I described my mental picture to Margie, she told me that Johnny owned a recreational type of vehicle that resembled a motorcycle but was used only in water. She continued, telling me that he had been in an accident on the Colorado River but thankfully had survived it because he was wearing a life jacket.

My senses were showing me that Margie was depriving herself of items she needed for herself, and I relayed this thought to her. She confessed to me that most of her clothing, as well as other items, had been purchased at garage sales. Margie admitted that she would not even indulge in the luxury of buying herself a new pair of shoes.

"The name Ronnie is being given to me. I assume that he is your husband," I continued. She told me that Ronnie was the name of her husband. I suggested to her that she was depriving herself of any new items because Ronnie was a gambler, both in risky businesses and horse racing. Margie agreed and admitted to me that she gave her husband far too much leeway with the money that they both earned.

I warned her to change her attitude regarding her self-image and attempted to show her that she deserved a better life than what she was currently experiencing. I continued by explaining that she needed to realize her own importance and should have been spending money on herself, and not feeling guilty about it. Margie's relaxed demeanor was going to make her bitter eventually and would turn her into someone who appeared to be a martyr with nothing being gained by anyone.

My psychic hearing was also telling me to encourage her to buy new items of clothing and not be fearful of taking a stronger stand with Ronnie regarding his lifestyle. Moderation is the key to success.

It's a message from you know where. Listen to it!

Pamela sat down for a reading and I heard music tones, in harmony and with a definite rhythm. She identified with what I said; she told me that she was a pianist.

I asked her why I was feeling legal issues and custody battles. Pamela told me that her former husband was taking her to court to fight for custody of her two teenage sons. I inquired about the name Hal. She reluctantly admitted to me that Hal was her ex-husband.

I told Pamela that I felt severe back pain for him. It was then that she came forth with the whole story. She explained that Hal had been badly injured in a car accident while driving home from work. A drunk driver hit his car, causing life-altering changes, disabling him for possibly the rest of his life. He could only lie in bed or on a couch because of the injury.

Then, Pamela tried to justify to me why she had divorced Hal. She explained that because he could not go on vacations or travel to any distant locations due to the pain in his back, her whole life had changed. His injuries also eliminated any trips to restaurants or social situations. This did not fit into her marriage plan.

I asked her about her marriage vows, which pledged staying together in sickness and in health. She ignored the question or just pretended that she didn't hear it.

Dismissing it doesn't make the issue go away. Injuries and illness can happen to anyone, including Pamela!

As soon as Bryan sat down for a reading, I felt that he had been abandoned and had no family. Bryan confirmed to me that his entire family had been killed in an automobile accident and that he had spent his childhood in an orphanage. He told me that he had lived those years feeling like a captive, with rigid rules and regulations. Bryan also admitted that he had been shunned by his peers because of his upbringing. I could actually feel the negative experiences he was speaking about.

He continued his story, telling me that he had fears of cancer, car wrecks, losing friends and pets, etc. He listed a variety of potentially anxiety-ridden thoughts that actually did not differ from the worries of many other people I knew.

Sad to Say (But Sometimes With a Happy Ending)

I told Bryan that his apprehensions were the same as almost everyone on earth and that I knew that he was a very kind, courageous and persevering person. I urged him to have positive thoughts and to be all the good things that he wanted to be. Eventually, things would get better. Promising activities were coming his way in the near future.

The light at the end of the tunnel is there, but you might have to look a little harder for it!

Lou sat down for a reading and immediately, I felt anguish regarding one of his children. I asked him who Ryan was and he told me that it was the name of his son. I knew that Ryan had been lured into the addictive world of drugs and alcohol. He was following in the tragic footprints of the rich and famous figures he admired. This boy's sad future was there for me to see and I needed to tell Lou that it was going to be a rough trip for both him and his son.

He sat there quietly, creating an awkward silence between us. Lou then stood up, embraced me and sincerely expressed to me his appreciation of my abilities. He needed to hear the real truth from someone without any false promises about drug and alcohol recovery.

Lou called me several months later and assured me that Ryan was in a rehabilitation center and was doing well. He told me that his son was very important to him and for that reason, Lou would not desert him.

My anonymous source says just to face the problem and deal with it!

I had never met Justine before but I knew from the moment that I observed her at the psychic fair that this woman had a lot of problems. I told her that the name Raymond was being given to me. She told me that Raymond was her husband. My feeling was that both Raymond and Justine were dealing with a tremendous amount of emotional pressure regarding a difficult decision that had to be made due to an unexpected pregnancy.

When I relayed this revelation to Justine, tears filled her eyes. She explained to me that she had just learned that she was pregnant and had no income or potential for any money in the near future. I told Justine that I didn't feel a house or apartment around them. She told me that they lived in a shelter.

I urged her to go to various government agencies for help. They were in a position to help her emotionally and monetarily.

I guess there is more privacy in a shelter than I thought!

Sandra sat down for a reading and I felt ups and downs around her involving an older woman by the name of Lillian. She explained to me that Lillian was her mother and was suffering from schizophrenia. This condition was very painful for Sandra to observe.

I could see Sandra on a television show in my mind's eye. She confirmed this by telling me that she was going to be auditioning shortly for a brand-new reality television show.

Maybe she would get the part. That would be exciting!

Sad to Say (But Sometimes With a Happy Ending)

When Ralph sat down for a reading, I immediately felt that he was anxious to speak about his daughter. I asked him if her name was Robin. Ralph acknowledged to me that it was her name and then asked me to tell him about her.

I told him that I could hear him shouting and threatening, which was a precursor to violence. I also mentioned that he was disconnecting from his daughter with this kind of behavior.

Ralph acknowledged what I said but then attempted to justify his behavior by saying that Robin was very difficult to control and that her tantrums were inexcusable. I expressed to Ralph that Robin was angry and afraid and was using this behavior to vent her frustration. She was insecure and needed to be listened to with respect. Respect, I informed him, is the foundation of a connection with anyone in our lives. Our most important parental task is to create a strong and lasting bond of love with our children.

Sometimes, the correct answer to a problem is so hard to implement!

As soon as Betty sat down for a reading, the name Susan came into my mind. Right after hearing that name, I heard the name Chris. I asked Betty what her relationships were to both of those names. She identified Susan as the name of her daughter and Chris as Betty's ex-husband.

I knew that I was given those two names to work with and focused on the feeling that there was an ongoing, contentious battle between Betty and Chris for custody of their daughter, Susan.

Betty verified my reading as correct. She assured me that she was currently spending many days in court trying to obtain full custody of Susan. I then sensed that Chris was acting inappropriately around his daughter, Susan. I could see in my mind's eye that he was showing his young daughter pornography on the Internet and in magazines.

When I said this, Janet admitted to me that Susan had mentioned that Chris was forcing her to watch pictures on the computer that made Susan feel uncomfortable.

Let's see what a judge will say about that one!

Katherine sat down with a fearful attitude regarding tarot cards. She told me that she didn't believe in them.

I promised her that I wouldn't use the cards if she had such a dislike of them. That made Katherine a little more comfortable, but she still seemed very angry. It didn't take me too long to figure out why.

Her next comment to me was that she was seeking to fulfill her destiny. I knew that she felt that her destiny included marriage. When I gave her the name Jimmy, she told me that this was the name of her boyfriend. She then told me that he didn't want to make a commitment to her because his mother was ill with cancer. He was waiting for her health to improve before he got engaged.

I advised Katherine to be strong and not give up hope on her dreams. It might not work out in the order she wanted it to, but her marriage destiny would come to pass.

My tarot cards would have told her the same thing!

When Ellen sat down for a reading, I could tell that she was a very timid person. I asked her who Jeanette was and she informed me that Jeanette was her mother. I had the feeling that Jeanette was blaming herself for Ellen's recent poor academic performance in school. Ellen expressed to me that her mom was devastated when it was grade determination time and Ellen received less than stellar marks on her report card.

In my mind's eye, I saw a pair of eyeglasses, so I asked Ellen if she wore glasses. She said that she didn't wear glasses, nor did she feel that she needed to. I told her to have her eyes checked as soon as possible because I was feeling that her grades were poor due to a vision problem.

A month later, Ellen called me on the phone to tell me that she had followed my advice and had her eyes examined. The eye doctor assured her that not only did she need glasses, but she needed them immediately. Now her grades are on the upswing. Ellen and Jeanette are both happy again.

Such a simple solution to such a common problem!

Jackie told me after he sat down for a reading that he had something very serious to discuss with me. Before he conferred with me about anything, I asked him if fifty yellow ribbons were indicative of a fifty-year celebration. He told me that his parents' golden wedding anniversary had recently been celebrated.

He then showed me a family photograph that contained his parents and siblings and asked me what I could ascertain from it. After looking at it, I saw that something was biologically incorrect. Everyone seemed to be totally part of the family except for Jackie. There seemed to be a partial disconnect there. I told him that I sensed that his mother was the only biological parent.

Attempting to hold back tears, he explained to me that he always instinctively felt that his father had never treated him the same way that he had treated the rest of Jackie's brothers and sisters. Jackie admitted that he had not been abused but rather ignored by his dad.

Unfortunately, I told him that his birth had been the result of an affair that his mother had prior to her marriage to his father. Jackie's face turned pale in response to this reading, but I had to be honest.

What makes a family a family?

Pamela called on the telephone for a reading. I had never previously spoken with her and was impressed by her candor.

I asked her who Linda was and she told me that Linda was her only daughter. When I told Pamela of a struggling feeling to empathize with her troubled adolescent, she verified my reading and then told me that it was all in vain. Pamela told me that Linda was suicidal and not agreeable to going for therapy.

I told Pamela to take her daughter to a family psychologist right away. For obvious reasons, being proactive is the only route in this type of situation.

Sometimes, as many of us already know, it is a hard road to adulthood!

Anita called me for a phone reading. My immediate thoughts went to embarrassing, revealing photographs of her that were in someone else's possession. I felt a damp, almost wet feeling from my neck up. I asked her if she could relate to these thoughts.

She said that she could, and revealed that her ex-boyfriend had the pictures I had mentioned and had spit in her face when she had ended the relationship. He refused to return the photos and Anita was quite disturbed about it. She feared that they would be placed on the Internet for all to see.

I was hearing the word *Philadelphia* and asked her what that meant. She then disclosed the name of her current beau, which was Phil. Another name came into my psychic hearing.

"Who is Sandy?" I asked Anita. She told me that her sister's name was Sandra.

Feeling a teenage boy around Anita, I asked her if she had a brother in that age group. She answered my question with a seemingly nervous "yes." I then went on to ask her about the issue of diapers. Anita was totally shocked that I knew that her brother had a diaper fetish.

She then explained that her mother was quite anguished over the fact that Anita's sibling was hiding diapers in his closet. When her mom had confronted him about it, he became defensive, embarrassed and annoyed at her invasion of his privacy.

Everything is out in the open in this one!

Chapter Ten

This and That

Linda came to me at a psychic party. The first question that I asked her concerned the number nine. What was the significance of that number to her? She casually disclosed to me that she had nine children.

But the interesting part of the story was that all the children had different fathers. Linda handed me photographs of the nine children and asked me who the fathers were because she had no idea. It was a real challenge, but I figured it out.

One thing that psychic work isn't, and that's boring!

Rochelle was a beautiful lady who I knew was very fascinated with metaphysics. I met Rochelle and her husband Ron at a psychic fair. They took turns coming to me for readings.

When Rochelle was sitting in front of me, I saw the energy, only visible to me, of an older man behind her pointing to his watch. I asked her the significance of it. She informed me that she had her deceased father's watch, which had been passed down to her after he died. When I asked her what the date October fifteenth meant along with the number forty, Rochelle was shocked. She told me that her father had died on October fifteenth and that it was going to be forty years since his death.

Her eyes filled with tears as she expressed her appreciation for my talent. She asked me how I knew all of this information. I explained to her that I had seen the date on a calendar. (Remember the prophesy regarding Grandma Mabel's death?) The "forty years" had been whispered in my ear.

I also asked Rochelle about a penny collection that I was seeing in my mind's eye. Rochelle informed me that the collection was something that her mother had for many years. The pennies were stored in metal tins that originally held cookies.

Because she was so open to being read and was such a believer, I was able to give her the names of both her parents' entire families. This absolutely thrilled and fascinated Rochelle.

When her husband Ron sat down for his reading, I asked him what the significance of pillows was. He explained to me that his mother used to collect them when she was alive. I was also able to tell him his parents' names as well as where they had resided when they were living.

Both Rochelle and Ron left the fair that day very excited because through me, they had contacted the other side of the veil. It was a new experience for them and one that would not soon be forgotten.

They referred dozens of people to me for readings because they valued my ability. This is truly the greatest compliment that any clairvoyant can receive.

When someone is open-minded and believes in metaphysics, it makes such a difference!

Emily sat down at my table for a tarot card reading. Before I even put the cards down, I apprised her of the fact that she was adopted.

Upon hearing this, Emily told me that she wasn't aware that she was adopted but wasn't surprised by the news. She continued, saying that she could never find her birth certificate when she needed it. Her adoptive father had revealed to her, while in a confused state days before his death, that she was his adopted daughter. She concluded her explanation by telling me that she was an only child and that her parents were considerably older than the parents of her friends.

She asked me who her biological parents were and where they lived. I was able to visualize through my psychic senses that her mother was a nurse and her father was a doctor. They had not been married and had not wanted to become parents when her birth mother became pregnant. I was also aware that they never did marry each other. Each found another spouse and Emily had a half sister from her mother. Her father never had any other children. They both lived in a Midwestern state.

Emily told me that she considered her adoptive parents her real parents. They had both been very generous and kind during her upbringing and although her father had passed, she could never hurt her mother by asking any questions regarding her adoption.

Sometimes, you can hear the messages and not act on them, but that's up to you!

Florence called me on the phone. She was a client who I had known for many years. She asked me for a general reading, meaning there was no specific issue on her mind.

As soon as I started meditating, I saw that there was going to be danger in her environment. This meant that Florence was going to have to be aware of the physical conditions and safety of her home. I definitely saw flames in my psychic vision.

Needless to say, she became very alarmed when I revealed to her the image I was seeing. Immediately, she asked me if her house was going to burn down to the ground. I assured her that I didn't feel that it would be a major catastrophe, but any fire, no matter how small, is a frightening thing to anticipate. My feeling was that the fire was going to start as a small electrical one. It would not be difficult to bring under control.

I suggested to Florence that she buy a fire extinguisher. I also warned her regarding the smoke alarm batteries in her home. They needed to be changed. She thanked me and we ended the session.

The following day, my phone rang early in the morning. I heard Florence's voice on the other end of the line. She told me that the electrical unit in her home's fish tank had caught fire. Fortunately, she was able to extinguish it and no one was injured.

Fire commands everyone's interest immediately!

A telephone call came in to the studio while I was working on talk radio. Sally wanted to know if she would become pregnant in the near future.

I knew that it was not humanly possible because my senses were telling me that Sally had been born a male, not female. I knew that she had undergone a sex change operation and was trying to test my credibility on the show.

I described to her my psychic vision and she confirmed it. At least we experienced a good laugh from it.

Now who's the believer!

Ellie called in to talk radio for a telephone reading. I felt as if she were redecorating her home, because a picture of the contents of her house being out of order came into my vision. She told me that she was currently having home improvements done by a contractor and that the workmen had just left.

I closed my eyes and became dizzy, which led me to my next statement regarding Ellie feeling faint. But, I also said that before she acknowledged that, I needed to know if something was in her eye. Ellie recounted to me that while the workmen were in her house, a sliver of wood had flown into her eye, which, for some reason caused her to have some dizziness. In fact, she had just gotten home from the doctor's office regarding this problem. Ellie's neighbor, John, had driven her to the doctor in Ellie's car because of the lightheadedness she was experiencing.

Then, I heard a gunshot in my ear. I asked Ellie about the noise and she said, while laughing, that her son, Roy, had been playing with his BB gun earlier in the afternoon and it mistakenly went off. A pellet hit her leg, leaving a scar. (I don't know what's funny about that.)

Then, a vision of keys came into my mind. I asked her if she had lost any. Ellie said that John, when exiting Ellie's car, had accidentally locked the keys inside. Ellie needed to wait until her husband, Wayne, came home because he had the spare key.

That reading sure was a busy one!

I was working at a psychic fair in one of the towns on Long Island when a woman approached me for a reading. She was wearing a face mask and refused to lift it up. To this day, and after many readings, I still don't know what she looked like.

I introduced myself to her and asked why she was wearing the mask. She explained to me that she wanted to be incognito. She then assured me that she wasn't famous. Her disguise was for protection regarding clues to my reading of her through facial expressions. Added to that, this woman refused to give me her name or her birthday, which I usually like to have prior to a reading.

Speaking in a barely audible voice, her speech was slurred. The little (and I mean little) that I could see of her face showed me no emotion. She requested that I not use tarot cards, so I closed my eyes to do a reading with no prior information and no tools.

Amazingly, I felt like I was sipping water and nibbling food on a spoon. It felt like I was sampling bites and savoring flavors. I suggested to this unique lady that I was feeling that she had odd dietary habits. She confessed to a lifelong eating disorder.

She must have been pleased with my reading because anytime that I appeared in this town at a psychic fair, she was waiting in line to see me, still wearing her mask. This went on month after month and year after year.

During one reading, when I questioned her regarding a connection to Georgia, she finally told me her name. Guess what? It was Georgia.

Talk about truth being stranger than fiction!

I was working on a talk-radio show and a listener by the name of Corinne called for a reading. She wanted to know about her finances for the coming year. The tarot cards showed a great deal of money coming to her but I didn't feel that her wealth was due to a job promotion or an inheritance. I felt the cash coming from a happening of good luck.

I usually don't tell people to gamble, however, my psychic vision was so strong that I encouraged Corinne to purchase a lottery ticket. She wanted to know the winning numbers. I suggested that she use family birthdays and anniversaries. I also told her to play bingo, go to the racetrack and visit a casino. Wealth for her was on the horizon. In essence, I prompted her to gamble in many ways, but in moderation, for one month.

Three weeks later, Corinne called to thank me. She had won over $2 million by playing the game Lotto. She asked me what she could do to show the appreciation she felt for my timely advice. I told Corinne to donate some of her winnings to charity and to give her friends my business card.

For months and months afterwards, my telephone was ringing constantly with calls from her friends who wanted readings. They, too, were looking to win big money. These individuals needed to realize that the message has to come to me. I don't control the winners or the winnings.

It was Corinne's destiny for her to call me so that I could deliver the message. In short, I was just the middle man—or, to be politically correct, the middle woman.

Beth came to me for a reading. I had never met her, but she had gotten my name from another client of mine. When I closed my eyes, I visualized splashes of color, paint, a smock, an easel and paint brushes. Needless to say, I saw her as a painter. When I told her about my intuitive feeling, she acknowledged that she was a freelance artist.

Beth was fascinated with my knowledge of her profession and asked me how I knew. I explained to her that my psychic vision showed me a picture of a pinwheel spinning around and around in a kaleidoscope of color.

I asked Beth if she had irregular eating habits. She answered that she was on a new diet program and wasn't really eating much in order to lose some weight.

Then, I started to hear the name and feel the presence of an older woman by the name of Rosemary around her. Beth told me that Rosemary was her deceased mother. This auditory message was followed by a picture of a calendar in my psychic visual field. The month of June was circled. I asked her what the relevance of that was. She informed me that her sister's name was June. Rosemary named her that because it was the month in which Beth's sister was born.

June is a pretty name. Thank goodness she wasn't born in October!

Vanessa called for a telephone reading. She was concerned about her son, Paul. He was about to graduate from high school but had no definitive future plans on his mind. He hadn't expressed any intention of attending college, nor did he know what type of career he was going to pursue.

While we were speaking with one another, I heard in my mind the words *moving out* coming through to me in my psychic hearing. This was definitely a message, so I asked Vanessa if Paul was moving out of the house just then. She told me that as far as she knew, he wasn't going to leave home until summertime.

I was ready to change to another subject when I heard noise coming from Vanessa's end of the telephone line. It was her son, Paul, entering the house. I heard him tell his mother that he needed to speak with her. She excused herself and turned her attention to her son. I was able to listen to the whole conversation because she did not realize that the speaker on the telephone was on.

"Mom, my friend Jason and I are renting an apartment. I'm moving out," said Paul to his mother. She asked him when he was leaving. "Now," he replied.

Vanessa picked up the phone to finish our reading and seemed absolutely shocked.

Looks like he means what he says!

Charlotte was a very strong, independent woman even though she was in her nineties. She came to me for a tarot reading and was very excited to hear what I had to say.

My immediate response to her tarot spread was that she was going in and out of the hospital even though she wasn't ill or a visitor. Her response to me was that I was correct. Charlotte was a hospital volunteer and in reality was feeling fine.

Charlotte's next question was really important. She asked me if she would be able to cease taking her medication, since she was feeling so well.

I adamantly advised her that she was feeling as well as she did as a result of being cared for by a physician. Only a professional doctor could tell her anything in regard to her treatment and medication. Psychics who are reputable will never tell a client to change, start or stop any health regimen prescribed by a medical practitioner.

Stick with your own specialty!

As soon as I met Sonya at a psychic fair, I smelled eggs and saw in my mind a full carton of twelve. When I asked what that meant to her, she admitted to me that the nickname given to her by her friends was Egg Nog.

She also mentioned with great pride in her voice that she had one dozen close friends. I chose to enhance that last statement with an observation from a strong vibe that I was receiving. I remarked to her that she was careful in her choice of friends and chose only those who brought prestige to her image. She told me that all of her inner circle of friends had professional occupations such as doctors and lawyers.

Talk about having specific requirements!

When Carrie sat down at the psychic fair, a vision of a car crash came into my view and I felt a suspension of her driver's license. Carrie told me that she had indeed been in an auto accident and that yes, her license had been suspended because she refused to take a sobriety test.

She then informed me that she was a college sophomore from New Jersey. I told her that I felt ink, but I didn't think that she was going to be a school teacher. She laughed and told me that she recently had a tattoo put on her shoulder.

Suddenly, in my ear I heard the song "Soldier Boy" and I asked her if she could relate to it. She told me that she was dating Tyler, an Army sergeant.

I can't think of a song regarding a tattoo!

When Renee came to see me for a private reading, I knew immediately that she was a successful and talented woman. I mentioned to her that my inner voice was telling me that she disapproved of her father's peculiar behavior.

Renee told me that her parents were divorced and her dad was currently dating a girl who was younger than Renee. She continued, telling me how embarrassing it was for her to think about the possibility of having a stepmother who was younger than herself.

My mind's eye immediately shifted at that time, showing me that Renee's mother was voluntarily having an operation about which Renee was upset. I inquired about this and was told by Renee that her mother was having gastric bypass surgery.

Nobody was cooperating with Renee!

Joseph came for a reading at a psychic fair and I was immediately struck by a vision of many females. I felt that there were three teenage girls and four grown women around him.

Joe told me that he had three daughters who were teenagers and four girlfriends who were pregnant with his babies. He thought that the whole situation was very funny because he denied responsibility for these pregnancies.

When I saw him laughing out loud, I chided him by saying that I didn't see any levity in the matter. Through his irresponsibility, he had ruined many lives. Did he forget that there are ways to determine if he was the father? He wouldn't be laughing for long.

This was a story of a warped sense of humor!

Lydia was shy and sweet, quietly asking me for a reading when she sat down. I saw a locket in my mind's eye and asked her about it. She told me that her mother had recently passed away, but had given Lydia a gold locket shortly before her death. Unfortunately, Lydia had lost it and was visibly upset, asking me if I knew where it was.

After revealing to her that my mind's eye was showing this specific piece of jewelry under the dining room table in her house, she looked totally relieved, if not flabbergasted.

Lydia left the reading with a sincere intent to find this locket. That evening, she called and breathlessly thanked me for helping her to find the keepsake that had been left to her by her beloved mother. She promised me with true sincerity that she would always treat it with special care.

A gift from someone who is now deceased is to be cherished forever!

Upon meeting Ellen at a fair, I felt "waiting and waiting." Ellen confirmed this feeling by telling me that she had been stranded at the airport after a major blizzard. Since all the nearby motels were filled, she was forced to sleep in a chair at the airport.

It was then that I heard the nursery rhyme "Little Tommy Tucker." She told me that Tommy was the name of her little son.

I should have asked her if he tucked her in at the airport!

Samantha, a woman in her forties, sat down and I was immediately struck with the fact that there was a pregnant teenage girl in her life named Jana, and Samantha was worried about her. Samantha informed me that Jana was her daughter. Samantha was quite concerned about the upcoming birth of her grandchild.

I asked Samantha who Joel was and she sarcastically answered that Joel was the father of Jana's baby. I then told Samantha about an upcoming wedding in the near future and this, too, was confirmed as the truth.

My next statement concerned a bachelor party that was disturbing to Jana. Samantha anxiously relayed a story to me regarding the celebration, which was given for Joel. It had become out of control when a female dancer who had been hired as entertainment became a little too familiar with Joel, who was, unfortunately, in a drunken state.

It sounds like this guy is quite mature, right?

Christine was a newlywed. When she sat down at the psychic fair, I thought of the lullaby "Rock-a-bye Baby." This was telling me that she was pregnant, and I told her so. Christine became very excited, saying to me, "Oh my goodness, you know that I'm pregnant."

I closed my eyes and saw a teddy bear. Christine said that her younger brother's name was Teddy and that she called him her teddy bear.

Well, you know who this baby's favorite uncle is going to be!

Sally called me on the telephone to express her anxiety regarding her husband's impending back operation, which was scheduled for the next morning. She was extremely nervous and was looking for me to reassure her regarding the operation's outcome. I expressed to her that I didn't feel that there would be any surgery the next morning.

Obviously perplexed, Sally told me that the pre-surgery testing was concluded and that everything was in order. She couldn't understand why I would feel that the surgery wasn't going to take place. But, I reiterated to her that the operation was going to be cancelled.

The next day, I received another call from Sally in which she informed me that her husband had been discharged from the hospital without having the operation. The surgeon wasn't able to be there because he had a family emergency.

It is what it is!

Joe sat down for a reading with me and I immediately felt that he had walked away from his family. He looked down at his hands and murmured that he had left a religious order to become a singer.

"Going on a blind date?" I asked.

"Yes, one of my friends is setting me up with someone in his office," Joe responded with a look of surprise.

"What happened in the diner that upset the waitress?" I asked next.

"Were you there?" he asked. I shook my head "no." He continued, telling me that he had to pay with coins for his meal because he had no paper money or credit cards with him.

"I only had coins, so I had to pay for the entire dinner with what I had. It took me a while to count it out and the waitress got very annoyed with me. Coins are still money, right?" He appeared to be looking for me to confirm his conviction that it really didn't matter how he paid for it, as long as he did pay for it. We both laughed.

When I asked him what the candles on the boat meant, he told me that his parents had given him a birthday party on a yacht.

Lots going on there!

Meryl was working as a physician's assistant. Her ultimate goal was to become a medical doctor.

As she was telling me this at the psychic fair, I asked her if she had a problem regarding her birth certificate. I felt that there was some type of confusion because she had not been born in a hospital or a house. In fact, it was undetermined where she was born.

Meryl confirmed these facts. She conveyed to me the anguish she endured regarding a request from a professor at the university she attended. He required her to locate the document. She told me that she had been born on an airplane in flight from Europe to the United States. She said that she wasn't even sure if she was a citizen of this country. Her parents did not know where the much-needed paper was. I assured her that her birth was recorded at the hospital she was taken to after the plane landed at the airport.

Then, I asked her who Patsy was. Meryl answered me that Patsy was her sister. I communicated to Meryl that I felt that Patsy's birth had also been out of the ordinary. I felt that she had not been born in a hospital either. Meryl smiled and explained to me with an embarrassed and hearty laugh that her sister had been born on a bus that was bringing her mother to the hospital.

At the end of the reading session, when Meryl was about to stand up, I asked her about a man whose name was Lloyd. She told me that Lloyd was her brother. I justified my question to her by saying that I don't like repeating myself but something was unusual about his birth, too. She told me that he also was not born in a hospital. He was born in a taxicab.

Meryl's mother apparently liked diversity in transportation while in labor!

When Melanie sat down for her reading at the fair, I immediately got specific vibes about her that all belonged together in a story. First I told her that I felt the letter A for a man around her. I followed this with the statement that there was a bottle of champagne, the number twenty-five, a celebration and patent leather. I prompted her to put all these things together in a story.

After putting her thoughts in order regarding my message, Melanie recited the affiliation of the information that I had given her. It started with the fact that her husband, whose name was Alfred, was just then at the liquor store buying champagne. Then, she disclosed that their twenty-fifth (silver) anniversary party was being held that night. She was going to wear a brand-new suit and her patent-leather boots for the occasion.

Here's to many more happy returns of the day!

When Sandra sat down at the table, I felt that there was an olive around her. She told me that her husband's name was Oliver.

Then, I started to feel that there was some type of trading happening with another couple whose names were Sally and Mickey. Sandra explained to me that she and Oliver had traded houses with another couple.

The other couple, Sally and Mickey, lived in another state and owned a small house but needed a larger one because they wanted to start a family. Since Sandra and Oliver were both recently retired, they felt that their house was too large for them to manage both financially and physically. It worked out for everyone.

I bet that you thought that I was going to say they were trading something else!

Rona and Artie were a married working couple who had no children. They came to see me at a psychic fair because of an ongoing problem that was happening in their house. Like most people, they were concerned about the high costs of owning a home, including the water bill, which is very often one of the cheapest expenses.

Artie began to realize that the water bills were becoming very costly. It didn't make sense to him that this utility bill was so high. He checked the faucets in the house for leaks and found no problems. He compared his water bill to his neighbor's and found that his neighbor, who had a larger family, owed less than he did. It was puzzling.

I asked Rona and Artie if they owned a cat, and they said they did. My mind's eye was showing me that the cat was sitting on the back of the toilet tank and continuously flushing the toilet while Rona and Artie were away at work. They both laughed and told me that the cat was never in the bathroom, so I suggested that they install a video camera.

The following week, I received a call from Artie, who told me that I was absolutely right. The video camera they had installed in the bathroom showed their cat flushing the toilet while Rona and Artie were at work.

Now the bathroom door gets closed before they leave the house each day. The cat needs to find something else to do to amuse herself and hopefully it won't cost her owners extra money.

Thank goodness for video cameras. Grandma Mabel, you were right. I am a detective!

Amy revealed to me that she had an unusual situation happening in her life. Before she told any more of her story to me at a psychic fair, I relayed to her my feeling that there were two men in her life, both of whose names started with the letter M. Amy told me that her husband's name was Marc and his father's name was Morton. I asked Amy who Charlotte was. She told me that Charlotte was the name of her mother.

It was then that I told her that I felt a strong connection between her father-in-law, Morton, and her mother, Charlotte. The feeling was one of being tied together.

Amy finished the story. She explained to me that her father and her mother-in-law had both passed away and Charlotte and Morton decided to marry. This made Amy and Marc not only husband and wife but also sister and brother.

Wow, linked in two ways!

Cassandra was wearing a Victorian-style dress when she came to the fair for a first-time reading. For some reason, I was immediately seeing the city of Paris, with a visualization of the Eiffel Tower. My view was inspiring to look at because it was sunset, which made it quite a romantic setting. I also saw sculptures and fountains in my picture of the city.

Of course, I asked her if she had a trip to Paris planned. She answered my question with a sigh and replied that she had just returned from France and had a wonderful time.

I asked her who Linda was. She smiled and informed me that Linda was her significant other.

I've never been to Paris but it must be lovely to see at that time of day!

Nathaniel, who had been married for more than thirty years, came to the fair for a reading. I asked him who Rosalind was and he told me that she was his wife.

I communicated to him that I was feeling a trip for him and Rosalind in the near future. I also conveyed my sense that there was adversity in their marriage. He confirmed both of these statements and then divulged to me that he was taking his wife to Paris because of the ongoing problems in their relationship. The purpose of the trip was to reignite the romance between them.

I hope he sees the Eiffel Tower the way I saw it! (See previous reading.)

It was New Year's Eve and I was the hired entertainment. Diane, who was wearing a sequined dress, walked into the room for a reading.

I asked her who Bernard was. She told me that Bernie was her husband.

Why was I seeing a yo-yo? She told me that she had spent her entire life yo-yo dieting. The scale would go up and down, up and down. She couldn't maintain her weight whenever she reached her goal.

How many of us can relate to that!

At the same party, Les came to my table for a psychic reading. The only clothing he was wearing was a tuxedo jacket and pants. I informed him of the name Tara, which I was hearing. He told me that she was his steady girlfriend.

Then, I asked him about the video of her pole-dancing, which Tara had given to him on Christmas Day, as his present. He calmly asked me if I had seen it. I told him that I saw it in my mind's eye.

Double wow!

Bonita was a little nervous when she sat down for a reading but not nervous enough to change her mind about following through with it. She asked me not to tell her any bad news.

I promised her that I didn't have any bad news to tell her and that I did feel someone around her whose name started with the letter K. She told me that her twin sister's name was Kate.

I heard the number five whispered in my ear and knew that it had some significance in Bonita's life. She disclosed to me that she had five children.

Then, I asked who in her family was middle-aged, wore cartoon socks and asked visitors to talk to his stuffed animals. She told me that she had a mentally handicapped brother named Jonathan. I suggested to her that I felt that Jonathan gives and receives happiness to all those with whom he is in contact.

I also informed Bonita that she was an inspiration to all because she never considered her brother a burden. In fact, she brought light into his life as well as the lives of everyone else she encountered.

Let people see that you are pleasant to be in contact with!

When Josephine sat down for a reading, I felt that she was overwhelmed by her busy schedule as a working mom. However, I was also hearing the name Harriet around her, who was possibly being of some help. Josephine commented that she was thinking of hiring a nanny her friend recommended—a woman by the name of Harriet.

If the name came up in the reading, then there was a good chance that Harriet would get the job!

Vera was anxious to meet me and was quite gracious when she sat down for her reading. I was honestly stunned when she introduced herself to me as an alien from another planet.

When I asked her about the accident, she looked around the room and then whispered to me that she had died in a car accident many years earlier and had come back to life. I asked her who Charles was and she disclosed to me that he was her brother who lived on another planet. Vera told me that she didn't see him too often for that reason.

And you think you have troubles...

After meeting Nanette at the fair, I asked her what the home project was about. She immediately told me about a "homemade type" bicycle she was constructing in the basement of her home.

Then, I began sensing that Nanette was very strong-minded. I sincerely felt that there was an issue she wanted to address with me but was uncomfortable doing it. I suggested to her that I felt a very sincere effort to overcome something. Nanette smiled and assured me that she had made a promise to herself that she was going to overcome prejudice. She revealed to me that her daughter was dating someone from a different background.

Save the strong mind for things you can change!

Jocelyn seemed very angry and depressed when she sat down for a reading. I could feel negative vibes radiating outwardly from her. She was serious and had no smile or greeting for me. Normally, I like to try to change that type of mood in a client, but it didn't seem as though she was going to be appreciative of my effort.

"I'm hearing the name Lenny," I informed her. She answered that Lenny was her boyfriend. I followed this statement by saying, "I'm also hearing the name Debra around the name Lenny." She then told me curtly that Debra was the name of Lenny's mother. I could tell from the tone of the answers that she was not going to enjoy her reading. She just appeared to be very tense.

I continued the reading by asking about a birthday cake about which she had been upset and disappointed. Finally, I had gotten through to her. Jocelyn's blank stare changed to an amazed, open-mouthed gaze. She was now thinking about something other than herself.

Finally, in a resolute but slightly quivering voice, she recalled for me the specific details of the anecdote concerning her birthday, which was on Christmas Day. She told me that she had been invited to Lenny's house for dinner. When she left the dining room after eating in order to make a telephone call, she returned to find a birthday cake on the table with candles on it. Jocelyn assumed that the cake was for her. When everyone started to sing "Happy Birthday," she was shocked that they were singing it to "baby Jesus" and not to her.

When Jocelyn mentioned to Debra that it was also her birthday, Debra said that Lenny had not even brought it to her attention. Debra then told Jocelyn that she was very embarrassed and felt very badly about not having a cake for her.

I pointed out to Jocelyn that it was actually a very funny story. She smiled and agreed.

Lighten up, everyone! There's enough birthday cake and celebration for everyone!

Cynthia came to see me for a reading at a psychic fair. When she sat down, I saw the colors red, white and blue, which made me think of the American flag and July Fourth. I inquired if she had experienced a serious accident on that date. She told me that she had an unfortunate horseback riding experience on Independence Day that had caused her to have four cracked ribs, a broken wrist and a broken leg.

I asked her what month her birthday was in. She answered that the month of her birth was December. I needed to know why I felt candles and cake in June. I was confused. She told me that her birthday was on Christmas day, and her parents felt badly that the holiday overshadowed Cynthia's special day, so they celebrated her birthday on June twenty-fifth.

Some dates you just can't change!

Here's another birthday story:

Denise looked depressed and I tried to determine what was bothering her when we sat together for her reading. I asked her if she was upset because people had forgotten her birthday. She told me that no one had forgotten about it. The problem was that everyone around her was just too hung over to celebrate it. She had been born on January first.

Trying to extract a better attitude from her, I encouraged her by saying that one of the advantages of being born on January first was that it was an easy date to remember.

She told me that she felt that her glass was half full. I assured her that her glass was more than half full. In fact, it was overflowing and she only needed to take a positive view of things. I explained to her that one of the encouraging things about being born on January first was that she probably would not ever have to work on her birthday. How many people can have that option on the anniversary of the day they were born?

January first—the start of the new year and the beginning of the rest of her life!

When Janice sat down for her reading, I began to feel that there was a house for sale and a raffle that needed to be won. I couldn't put the two together, so I asked Janice what it all meant.

She relayed the story, which actually evolved as a reflection of the real estate market being as it was. Since houses were difficult to sell, Janice had a bit of a problem because she needed to obtain a certain price for her house. Her real estate agent was finding it difficult to find a buyer willing to spend anything resembling the asking price of Janice's house.

When the contract expired with the agent, Janice decided to sell raffle tickets for $100 each. The winner of the raffle would become the owner of the house. She sold 5,000 tickets and one year later, Janice was able to give her house to the lucky person who won.

I then questioned Janice regarding someone by the name of Danny. She proudly informed me that Danny was her young grandson. I asked her why I was seeing a fearless comic book character in my psychic vision. She told me that Danny was a daredevil. He wasn't afraid of adventure. In fact, he loved taking chances.

I wonder if Danny would have bought a house raffle ticket for $100!

I met Gerry at a psychic party. I was feeling that he had undergone emergency surgery on a holiday. Gerry corrected me by saying that the operation had not occurred on a holiday but rather on his fortieth birthday. He told me that he and his wife had made plans for a large birthday bash, which had to be cancelled.

Then, Gerry asked me if I knew where on his body the surgery had been done. My senses were telling me that it was in the head and neck area, and I conveyed that to him. He verified my reading by saying that the procedure had been done on his vocal chords. He was a professional singer.

I hope the doctor was able to sing "Happy Birthday"!

Jeremy was a young man who was very excited about his first tarot reading. I asked him who Shelly was. He identified Shelly as his wife. Then, I asked him who Ralph was. He told me that Ralph was a friend of his. I told Jeremy that he, Shelly and Ralph all had something in common in regard to their birthdays.

Jeremy chuckled as he explained the story to me. It seemed that he had met Shelly at his friend Ralph's birthday party. While Jeremy and Shelly were conversing with each other, Jeremy informed her that his birthday was also on that day. Shelly then divulged to Jeremy that her birthday was on that day, too. The end result of this mutual revelation was that the three of them had been born on the same date in different years.

You always feel a kinship with a stranger born on the same date as you were!

Mary attended a psychic fair and disclosed to me that she had never had a tarot reading. She asked me if I could only tell her good things because she was frightened of predictions that might give her unfortunate forecasts.

I asked Mary if she had a twin sister and if her twin sister sang karaoke. She confirmed that she did have a twin sister and that her sister was an enthusiastic karaoke singer. However, she continued, her sister was actually an opera singer. I asked Mary who Deborah was. She said that Deborah was the name of her twin sister.

That was certainly pleasant enough!

Antoinette walked toward me at the fair and I sensed the aroma of flowers. I also saw a tremendous amount of roses and many vases in my psychic vision. I asked Antoinette who Bart was. She identified Bart as her husband.

Antoinette then acknowledged that her husband had given her fifty red roses for their golden wedding anniversary, but she did not have a large vase in which to put them. She looked around her house and found many small vases, and she used them to hold the huge quantity of flowers that her loving husband had bought for her.

It certainly does make it easier to distribute the lovely fragrance around the house!

Beverly, Toby and Janet came together and wanted me to do a reading for all of them. I didn't want to leave anyone out of the reading, so I tried to see what they all had in common.

My reading of them concerned some type of vaccination they had received after attending an anniversary party. They all laughed hysterically. I had hit on something that was actually true. The story Beverly told me was that one of the waiters had an active case of hepatitis and all the guests were told to see a doctor immediately.

That's not such a good thing to have in common!

Annette sat down for a reading wearing a chain around her neck with a large, gold crucifix on it, but I kept hearing Jewish songs. When I questioned her about this, she told me that she had tried out for a chorus but was rejected, so she tried out for a Chanukah chorus and happily, she had been accepted into it.

I asked her who Carl was. She said that he was her boyfriend.

Everybody, including Carl, should sing along!

After meeting Diane at a psychic fair, I sensed that she held an important management position, but I also felt that she was not a tough person. To me, she seemed to be a woman of compassion with a kind nature.

When I asked her what the reunion was about, Diane told me that she and her brother were estranged from each other and that they were reconnecting because their elderly mother had to be taken care of.

This mother must have been happy to see her children reunited!

Larry and Dina came for a reading together. They had met years earlier and now lived and worked in Spain.

I saw in my psychic vision that they were house hunting, but at the same time, they were not planning to move. When

I informed them both of what I was feeling, Larry excitedly indicated to me that they wanted to buy a vacation home on Long Island, which was close to water and near Dina's family. Dina then chimed in enthusiastically, saying that they were looking for a house with a "breathtaking view."

Breathtaking views are for me. Maybe they'll invite me to the new house when they find it!

Marcia was dressed in a disguise, consisting of a wig, a big hat and dark sunglasses, when she walked over to me at a psychic fair. I asked her if she was a celebrity. She told me that she was a famous actress and was wearing these theatre aids so that no one would recognize her.

I indicated to her that I felt horses and trails around her. She explained that she had just purchased a ranch in Wyoming, where she planned to take up residence when she retired.

I was also feeling that heart disease was prevalent in her family. She cautiously looked around and quietly assured me that I was correct in my assessment. Continuing on, she divulged to me that that her father and brother had been diagnosed with it and both were embarking on personal quests to learn more about the efforts that would eventually lead to a cure.

People think that being rich and famous guarantees you everything in life—but it doesn't!

Anna was an Iranian girl who wanted a psychic reading very badly. She came to a fair and I immediately sensed that she was dressing up in some type of costume without her parents' knowledge.

Anna acknowledged that she was forbidden to watch soccer, so she was dressing as a man and going out to view local games without her folks knowing about it.

Talk about enthusiasm for a sport!

Megan, a young teenager, was quite excited about her first reading. I felt that she was too concerned about her weight even though she was thin and petite. When I asked her about this, she told me that she wanted to lose ten pounds.

I also started to feel something about cosmetic surgery, which she answered in the affirmative. She had a rhinoplasty procedure—a nose job—performed by a renowned plastic surgeon.

Then, I asked Megan something that was not given to me psychically. I asked her why she had applied such a large amount of make-up on her pretty face. She answered that she needed more plastic surgery and she was trying to hide any flaws in her face with heavy cosmetics.

Megan, in my view, was absolutely adorable, but she had to be the one to see it—and she obviously didn't!

Murray chose me as his tarot reader and told me that a lot of thinking had gone in to his decision. He had made his choice as he stood outside the room watching all the readers. He never gave me a reason why he chose me, but I guess he just used his intuition.

I told him that my psychic vision was telling me that he was studying tarot at home. I felt that he was determined to learn the interpretive meaning of each card himself.

Murray confirmed what I was feeling. He went on to say that he practiced being "still," but no matter how hard he tried, he never heard any voices inside his head.

I told him that when he was totally willing to hear the voice from the anonymous source, it would be spoken to him. I recommended that he attempt to reach the power he was looking for during the early hours of the morning. This was the ideal time to reach out in order to learn his purpose in life, and it could be done through meditation.

Everyone should try it. What have you got to lose?

Roberta came for a reading and I knew immediately that this was a woman who was picayune about all kinds of things. I asked her if she was known to make mountains out of molehills. I felt that Roberta needed to learn to keep a correct perspective on problems and not blow them out of proportion beyond their real worth.

Sensing that she was continually angry, I was drawn to the fact that her wrath was usually vented as criticism of any and all things as well as people—which included her family. But, I was also feeling that her relatives were getting tired with and disgusted by her behavior.

Roberta candidly admitted to me that she liked to point out the flaws of others. She then said that she was well aware of the fact that the members of her family were the only ones who would tolerate her behavior. Unfortunately, she was not deterred from making her comments even though she was conscious of how unhappy it made everyone.

I urged her to apologize to those she was constantly finding fault with because there were plenty of things that they could criticize in her. I also said that she needed to find a less stressful way of life, which she constantly craved.

Watch what you say and do. What goes around comes around!

Samantha came for a first time reading and I felt that there was a parking ticket on her mind. Immediately, she knew what I was speaking about and recounted a story to me concerning a law enforcement officer who had given her a summons for parking her automobile in a handicapped parking space. Since she had no physical disabilities, she did not have the proper sticker on her car. Samantha vowed to me, in no uncertain terms, that she wasn't going to pay the ticket. She planned on disputing it in court.

I asked her who Vinnie was. She told me that he was the person who had parked her car in the handicapped spot. She had allowed him to drive the vehicle while she was in the passenger seat. He had left her sitting in the car while he went into a store to purchase a cup of coffee for himself. Unfortunately for Samantha, the automobile was spotted by the officer and the ticket was issued.

I told her that it was the wrong thing to do. If you break the law, you deserve a ticket.

Handicapped parking spots are for the disabled. Enough said!

When Danny sat down with me for a psychic reading, I had the impression that he was surrounded by cement canyons. Danny's answer to that feeling was that he worked in Manhattan.

I sensed fresh air, open spaces, sports, driving ranges and competitions. Danny disclosed to me that he intended to enter a golf tournament.

When I asked Danny who Marty was, he identified him as his golf partner. Then, I asked who Jessica was. He answered that Jessica was his bride to be.

The golf partner came out in the reading before the bride to be… Hmm!

I felt a pregnancy around Sandy when she sat down for a reading. I also sensed multiple illegal drugs and prostitution.

Sandy admitted to me that although I was correct, she was no longer a drug addict or a prostitute. She had given them both up for the sake of her unborn baby.

I felt a man around her by the name of Leo and asked who he was. She told me that Leo was the name of her baby's father.

It's good news when people turn their lives around!

I could hear a beautiful singing voice around Millie when she sat with me for a reading, but I also knew that she was writing a song instead of singing one.

When I asked her about this, Millie admitted to me that while she did have an exceptional voice, she couldn't find anyone who was able to write an original piece of music for her to sing. For that reason, she had decided to write her own song.

Millie then conveyed to me, with much excitement and passion, how enjoyable it was to write songs. After expressing her plan to compose original material, she told me that any creative arrangement she would record would have to meet strict requirements—something she always required in any of her endeavors.

I asked Millie who the older woman by the name of Jenny was. She clarified my reading by telling me that Jenny was her recently deceased grandmother.

A psychic message was whispered in my ear, and I told Millie that Jenny was with another person by the name of Rose. Millie explained to me, with tears in her eyes, that Rose was Jenny's sister. Millie assured me that it was comforting for her to know that Jenny and Rose were together now, as they had been in their lives on earth.

Jenny and Rose will appreciate the song that is waiting to be written and sung!

Mario sat down with me for a reading and I felt hundreds of cars around him. He smiled and said that he worked in a New York City garage as a parking attendant.

I suggested to Mario that my senses were telling me that he was grieving over a woman. He answered me, in a low voice, that he had just become a widower.

When I informed him about a large party that was looming in the near future, he told me that he was in charge of organizing a high school reunion. At first, he hadn't wanted to take the project on, but after thinking about it, he had decided to do it.

I asked Mario who was house hunting in Italy. Mario explained that his parents were looking in a certain region in Italy for a structurally sound residence that they could use as a vacation home. They wanted it to be spacious enough for visits by the entire family, which consisted of their five children, their children's spouses and their grandchildren. I told Mario that I could see vegetables in my mind's eye, and he told me that his parents wanted to have enough land to grow produce.

From a parking garage in New York City to a vegetable garden in Italy—certainly a diverse lifestyle!

After meeting Miriam at a psychic fair, I sensed a lot of firsts around her. When I told her that, she asked me what I meant. I disclosed to her that I felt a first pregnancy and a first house, and she admitted that I was correct on both issues.

I also suggested to Miriam that she was thinking of becoming a stay-at-home mom because she didn't want to put her child in daycare. I added from my psychic knowledge that there was a possibility that she might change the basement of her house into an apartment that she could rent out. This would enable her to have a new source of income, since she wasn't going to be working.

Miriam put her hand to her mouth in disbelief and disclosed to me that she had just been discussing that proposal with her husband during the car trip to the psychic fair.

She wasn't the first to react like that during a reading!

Jane walked over to me and requested that I read her cards. In response, I asked her if she was a newlywed. She was very surprised that I knew this fact because she was in her sixties.

I was sensing that Jane was going to be moving. She told me that she and her new husband wished to move out of the studio apartment in which they lived. They needed a two-bedroom apartment because of a mutual desire to have more space in which to live.

I asked her who Larry was. She identified Larry as a member of her family for whom they were seeking domestic intervention. Larry was having a problem with alcohol.

I don't know which side of the family Larry was on, but it was an important enough issue that I was told about it!

When Melissa sat down for a reading, I was immediately sure that she was making improvements to her house that had turned into a costly nightmare. When I asked her about it, she told me that she had purchased a house that had been listed as a "handyman special." Melissa said she had known that her residence needed work, but she didn't realize how much money she would have to spend to improve it inside and out.

I expressed to Melissa that I felt tunnels around her. She smiled and answered that she was an MRI technician and the equipment she used looked like a tunnel.

No comfortable surroundings for her!

Sam came to me for a reading at a psychic fair. I was feeling a love interest around him by the name of Laura. He told me that Laura was his fiancée. He had recently become engaged to her.

I was also getting a psychic impression that he was hoping to purchase a house and had recently found one he considered a bargain. Sam confirmed my reading, explaining to me that there was a foreclosed townhouse that he and Laura were considering buying.

I made clear my feelings that due to a creative imagination, Sam had a talent for writing children's stories. He disclosed to me that he had just finished writing an adventure book for youngsters.

His life was on track!

Stella was an animal lover and I knew it from the start of the reading. I asked her how many animals she had in her home. She admitted to me, with pride, that she had five cats and two dogs.

I also felt that she was having a difficult time finding an affordable apartment that would accommodate all of her pets. I could sense that this had been an ongoing problem for a while.

Stella went on to explain that whenever a potential landlord would find out about all of the animals, the rental arrangement would be negated and she would be back to apartment hunting again. I suggested that she get a specialist in real estate to help her with her problem.

It's a shame that animals don't own houses. Then, they could refuse to rent to people unless they owned pets!

Bret sat down for a reading, but when he gave me his name, I asked him if it was his middle name. He explained to me that he used his middle name because he didn't like his first name. I questioned him regarding his first name. Was it Carey? He told me that it was.

Then, I visualized in my mind's eye that he was a military veteran. This he proudly answered in the affirmative.

When I revealed to Bret that I felt a big move in his future, he told me that since being discharged from the Army, he had been living in the basement of his brother's house. Now, he had finally accumulated enough money for a down payment on a home of his own. He was in the midst of purchasing a house on Long Island.

Welcome aboard!

Julia called in to a talk-radio show for a reading. I asked her if she wanted to join a sorority at her college. She told me that she wanted to be involved in such a club very badly. I then suggested to her that I felt that there would be a very harsh hazing for her.

She admitted to me that although she wanted to participate in the organization along with the rest of the girls, she feared what the members would do to her in the standard initiation into the group. Julia had a difficult decision to make.

I explained to her that if these girls planned to abuse her, then they were not really her buddies. Julia would be better off finding another way of obtaining relationships and inducing camaraderie.

Life can be painful enough—don't voluntarily add more to it!

Chapter Eleven

She/Her and He/Him

I met Ray at a psychic party. He told me that his wife had recently disappeared, and he was wondering if he should report it to the police.

Immediately, I saw flashing lights and heard bells ringing, which showed me that she was in a casino. I told this gentleman that his wife hadn't been kidnapped. She was away with someone she had met online, on her home computer.

I then advised him that the man who was with his wife was not only using her for sex but also for money, which she was getting from Ray's credit cards. I advised Ray to cancel all his credit cards immediately and assured him that his wife would be back after the new boyfriend spent all of her money—or, should I say, Ray's money. But, I also warned him that she was going to repeat this behavior and that Ray shouldn't be caught off guard again.

A month later, a grateful Ray called to thank me. He told me that his wife did come back, but he was not going to let her make a fool of him a second time. He was through with her because everything contained in my psychic reading in reference to the situation was correct.

Ray wasn't going to be deceived twice in one lifetime if he could help it!

Not too many readings leave me speechless, but the following one certainly did.

Just when I thought that I had heard it all, I met Dana. I introduced myself and handed her my tarot cards to shuffle. Upon putting the cards on the table in front of me, I informed Dana that her husband had a secret and that the situation she found herself in required a lot of personal sacrifice on her part.

I then told her that her husband loved her and wanted to stay married to her. The problem was that he wanted a sex-change operation.

Dana verified my reading, telling me that I was absolutely correct. She and her husband had been married for twenty-four years, but he felt that he had been born the wrong gender.

How many people could make such a sacrifice?

When I was a guest on a talk-radio show, a listener named Henry called in. He sounded very upset over his wife's unusual hobby. Immediately, I saw in my mind's eye that his wife was dressing as a drag queen.

Excitedly, Henry yelled, "Bingo!" He said that his wife was impersonating a man dressing as a woman and going to gay bars. This eccentric behavior was putting their marriage in jeopardy because as Henry phrased it, "She is not meeting my expectations." He told me that her hobby was a complete embarrassment to him.

You never know what goes on behind closed doors—and maybe you don't want to!

Another radio show story was somewhat accurate, but with a change of players.

Rick called me and I immediately felt an obsession with recreational contests. My question to him was regarding his children and if any of them were guilty of this.

He laughed and told me that he had no children, but his wife had an obsession with video games. Her hobby was causing marital conflicts.

Some things just don't have age boundaries!

While sitting in a television studio, I received a telephone call from Troy. The sound of his voice brought legal issues and theft to my mind.

Troy explained to me that he was renting out an apartment in his house and that the tenant, a young woman, had stopped paying rent because she had lost her job.

When Troy threatened to take legal action against her, she assured him that she would retaliate by reporting him to the Internal Revenue Service for renting an illegal apartment. Troy was concerned that he would have to pay extra taxes and interest.

I suggested that he sell the house. This might have solved his problem because the tenant would be forced to move. He thought my suggestion would solve the problem and told me that he would do just that.

She still could have reported him. Sometimes, there are no correct answers!

I met Roxanne in 1994 at a psychic fair. She explained to me that she had been dating a young man named Adam since high school. She was deeply in love with him but had turned down his marriage proposal. Her reasons seemed honest and, in a sense, logical. Roxanne wanted to live on her own for a while before marriage. She wanted to travel and have freedom, and she was not going to be dissuaded from it.

Unfortunately, Adam did not want to wait. He was ready to begin his life with her right away. He gave Roxanne an ultimatum. Roxanne felt very confused and unhappy. She assured me that there was a feeling in her heart that they were soul mates and meant to be together.

With all of this in mind, I asked her to shuffle the tarot cards, which, when laid out for reading, expressed to me that if Roxanne married Adam under that type of pressure, she would feel anger and regret. My advice to her was not to suppress her desire to travel the world.

But, I had good news for her, too. I advised Roxanne to attend her ten-year high school reunion because Adam would be attending also. Not only would he be there but he would be there alone, waiting for her. Roxanne replied with a happy scream. She said it sounded incredible, that it would never happen because it was too perfect an ending. "Life doesn't work out so easily," she said.

In 2004, ten years later, Roxanne returned to me for another reading. The tarot cards told me that she had attended the reunion and as predicted, Adam had been there alone.

Both had remained single and after dating for a short time, they were now planning a wedding.
You can have your graduation cake and eat it, too!

Marty sat down with me for a reading because he wanted to know about his wife, Suzanne. He suspected that she was cheating on him. Due to the fact that he worked nights, he was unable to track her whereabouts while he was away from her. Whenever he called home, she wasn't there. Suzanne always had various reasons for not being home and it was hard for Marty to dispute them.

Another thing that bothered him was that Suzanne continually requested extra money from him. Marty told me that Suzanne wasn't a real shopper, and therefore he wanted to know what she wanted the money for.

I did a reading on the situation and suggested to Marty that Suzanne was at church. He told me that my answer was not rational because he and his wife were both Jewish. I promised him that I would meditate on it again, which I did. Once more, my psychic message came up the same way: Suzanne was at church. Marty left seeming very annoyed by me because my answer did not make any sense to him.

The next day, he called me on the telephone and giddily informed me that he had left work early and followed his wife, only to discover she was going to the local church to play bingo. She needed the money to play the game.

Marty was probably relieved that this was the game she was playing!

Ella came to me for a reading. The tarot cards showed much tension and worry about money. Even though her marriage was strong and solid, I felt that Ella's husband was prone to gambling without her knowledge.

This news upset Ella because she was working six days a week and doing all the housecleaning, errands and other chores. She was resentful of his selfishness.

After my reading, Ella confronted her husband, and he admitted to it. He promised her that he would stop and he did, because Ella periodically calls me to check on him. Now there is more money in the bank account and there is a cleaning service at her house.

They both (hopefully) lived happily ever after!

As soon as Kyle sat down with me for a reading, I could hear a clock ticking. Then, I heard "cuckoo, cuckoo." I asked him if he could relate to this. Kyle said he owned a clock repair shop. He then abruptly informed me that he hadn't come to see me for a discussion of clocks.

The purpose of his visit was for me to give him lottery numbers. I explained that if I knew the winning numbers, I wouldn't be sitting there giving readings to clients. (Even though I have been given some messages regarding gambling, as you have already read, I never know when such messages will come to me.)

Since I couldn't give him any lucky lottery picks, he asked me about how fortunate he would be with his love life. This I was able to tell him. I informed him that I felt several relationships in his future. The name Kim came immediately into my mind.

Kyle explained to me that Kim was his first true love, but she had ended their relationship. She had made the decision to leave him when it was clear to her that he was leaving her out of his outside activities and was drinking too much. Kyle admitted that he still had intense feelings for her and hadn't really accepted the demise of their relationship.

Happily, I was able to tell Kyle that Kim never married and that she was still in love with him. This news was something of a relief to him.

Several months later, I received a phone call from him, telling me that he and Kim had reconciled and were once again together.

The rest was up to them. I am just the messenger!

Immediately upon meeting Cynthia at a fair, I thought of a well-known amusement park. Cynthia told me that the reason I was getting that feeling was that her life had been a rollercoaster, with lots of ups and downs.

I advised her that I felt that she was dating men who were not available to take the final step of marriage. Cynthia admitted to being afraid of intimacy and so was only dating men who were unobtainable or preoccupied.

Suddenly, I smelled lamb stew and felt that there was a man around her with two Js. She told me that currently she was dating a man named Joe, whose last name also started with a J. He was working as a chef in a local restaurant.

I am appreciative when more than one of my senses kick in to help tell the story!

Paige came to a psychic fair for a reading. From the moment she sat down, I felt that her life was surrounded by chaos and dysfunction. When I brought the name Chelsea into the conversation, Paige became visibly upset. I told her that I felt that a woman by this name was sneaky, with malicious intentions. Paige revealed to me that Chelsea was trying to lure Paige's husband out of their marriage.

Suddenly, I saw piles of shirt buttons in my mind's eye. When I asked Paige the significance of this, she told me that when she had discovered what was happening with her husband and Chelsea, she cut all the buttons off of his shirts.

Then, the name Warren was whispered into my ear. When I informed Paige of this, she told me that Warren was her husband's name. I then started feeling patterns around Warren, meaning that this behavior was not unusual for him. When I informed Paige of this revelation, she explained that Warren had an ongoing routine of having affairs. My next question was in regard to the names Maureen and Jennifer. Paige told me that these were two women with whom she had previously contended during her marriage to Warren.

Then, I heard the name Monique. Paige told me that Monique was the woman to whom Warren had previously been married. I heard the name Janet. This woman, Paige informed me, was the one for whom Warren had left his first wife.

The name Yvonne was also whispered into my ear. Yvonne, Paige told me, was Warren's sister. Then, finally, my psychic hearing sense gave me the name Sherry. Paige told me that Sherry was Warren's boss.

Certainly a busy guy!

Bonnie called me for a telephone reading. She had gotten my name from another client of mine and was very curious about psychic readings.

I heard the name Steve around her. She told me that Steve was the name of the man she was going to marry in a few months.

My feeling was that Steve liked to be first in anything that he attempted. I also felt that he liked to explore—he enjoyed being a pioneer. I cautioned Bonnie that since he was that kind of person, he would never ask for help with anything. I expressed to her my perception that driving directions were a real problem with him. He would rather find the location himself, even if he were hours late.

I knew that this stubbornness was causing problems between the two of them. Bonnie agreed and told me that punctuality was very important to her, and it was for that reason that she had chosen to do a phone reading. She was fearful that if she had a reading in person and he couldn't find the location, she would be late. This was very troublesome for her.

I advised Bonnie that she should get her own driver's license. Bonnie was shocked that I knew that she did not have a license, since most people in her age group had already obtained one. She admitted to me that nothing was within walking distance of her home. Someone always had to drive her.

After the reading, Bonnie thanked me and said that she decided to get her own driver's license. She was not going to be dependent on anyone to get her anywhere on time.

Nothing like being independent!

Al walked up to my table at a psychic fair and immediately, I knew that he had a secret. He was having an extramarital affair.

I told him I heard the name Liz and he replied that this was the name of his wife. The name Annie and the word baby were also whispered in my ear, so I quickly repeated them to him. Al confirmed what I was hearing, telling me that his wife had recently given birth to a baby whom they named Ann-Marie. However, he called her Annie.

There were two more names ringing loudly in my ear: Barbara and Vera. Al told me that his mother's name was Vera and that she had recently discovered that Al was having an affair with Barbara. I asked him if the affair was partially due to Liz's weight gain.

Sheepishly, Al admitted that Liz had gained a considerable amount of weight during her pregnancy, causing him not to be attracted to her anymore. He defended his actions by saying that Liz was quite busy taking care of the baby and was therefore too tired to be intimate with him.

I suggested that he end the affair and instead of finding excuses for his straying, he should help his wife so that she would be more inclined to concentrate on her appearance. Her tiredness could also disappear if there were someone to share the responsibilities of taking care of Annie. Al had no comment, but he certainly appeared to feel guilty.

If you look for a reason, you will eventually find one to substantiate your position on an issue!

Carrie was very tense when she met me—until the tarot cards predicted a happy future for her and her fiancé, Nick. She then conveyed to me her apprehension that the wedding they had planned would never come to pass because Nick had already cancelled and then rescheduled the date.

I told her that this time the wedding would be realized because Nick was ready to make the move. I felt the closeness of the two of them. There was some anger between them because of the postponement, but Carrie called me several weeks later and informed me that the wedding had indeed taken place.

Nervous for no reason!

When Cameron sat down at my table, I was quite impressed by his appearance. He was dressed very well and was indeed a handsome man to look at. Immediately, I felt two sisters around him, both with names that started with the letter E. He told me that he had no sisters, only one brother, but he admitted that he was dating two sisters at the same time. Neither one of them had knowledge of his involvement with the other.

I asked him who Erica and Emma were. Cameron informed me that these were the names of the two sisters. Erica lived in Manhattan and Emma lived on Long Island.

The Christmas holiday was approaching, and he feared that the secret life he was living would be exposed for all to see. After looking at my tarot cards, I revealed to Cameron that they said he was walking on the wild side and would soon be walking alone in the dark.

Don't these sisters talk?

Alicia called me early one morning for a telephone reading. She had a story concerning the devastation she was feeling due to a young man for whom she had strong feelings. He refused to commit to a relationship with her. I asked her if his name was Donald and she confirmed that it was.

She continued her story, referring to Donald as a womanizer whom she just couldn't rein in. I saw in my mind the letter K. Alicia told me that Donald's latest love was named Kate. Alicia then said that she had begun to come to terms with the fact that Donald was not a one-woman man. She was now realizing that the best route for her was to move on with her life.

I was happy to tell her that I felt a new man coming into her life; his name started with the letter J followed by three other letters, such as Jack or Josh. One week later, Alicia called to tell me that she had met two men, one named Jack and the other one named Josh.

Just assess the situation and do what you have to do!

Ryan was an emotional con artist who could convince anyone to do anything. My feeling, after meeting him at a fair, which I conveyed as discreetly as possible, was that he was a drug addict. He confirmed it, speaking in a practically inaudible voice. But, he then suggested to me that his real addiction was to a former girl friend.

I told him that I felt two women around him, one named Jacqueline and the other named Elizabeth. Ryan disclosed to me that Jacqueline was the one he was deeply in love with, but she had left him because of his substance abuse problem. He was currently dating Elizabeth, but Jacqueline was the one with whom he was totally enamored.

Girlfriends and drugs are not a good combination!

When Paula sat down with me for a reading, I saw in my mind canvas, paint brushes, paint and artwork along with pictures and plaques. I felt that she was a decorator, which she verified was a fact.

Then, I psychically saw a man with a bulletproof vest and a target on his face. I also saw in my mind's eye a shield with a number. I told Paula, "There is a police officer in your life and his name is Christopher. I'm also seeing a maxed-out credit card borrowed from someone else, which you used. It caused hard feelings, bitterness and animosity with the person whose card it was. Actually, I'm seeing it as belonging to Christopher's mother, and I'm being told that she is taking you to court because of it."

Paula seemed very embarrassed by my statement and while choosing to ignore my last vision, said, with an uncomfortable smile, that Christopher was her longtime boyfriend. She quickly added that he was in law enforcement. Paula told me that she was tired of waiting for Chris to propose and felt that his mother was the person who was discouraging him from tying the knot.

Maybe the judge who does the sentencing can also perform the marriage ceremony!

Without telling me details, Collette admitted that she had a difficult childhood, but when she sat in front of me at a fair, she appeared confident and lovely, with a smile to match. She was successful in her job and was moving on with her life.

She began the reading by informing me that she was getting married. I was feeling pre-wedding jitters, which is not unusual, but in this case, it was extraordinarily stressful.

Collette confessed that she was getting a little anxious concerning her marriage because she felt that she really didn't know her husband to be, Neil, well enough. The nuptials had been planned after a very short time dating, and she was having some doubts about the wisdom of this.

It was then that I saw commuter trains in my mind's eye. Collette informed me that this was showing me Neil's occupation—he was a train conductor.

Suddenly, I had a vision of a certain television show in which the main character was a mischievous little boy. When I asked her who Dennis was, she told me that Dennis was Neil's son from a former marriage. She added that Dennis was indeed a curious and active child while going through the terrible two's stage.

So much to know, so much to know, so much to know!

Erin was a beautiful woman. She sat down with me for a reading and I soon discovered that she had a wonderful sense of humor.

After speaking with her for a short time, I informed her that I was hearing the name Jacob around her. With a huge grin on her face, she told me that Jacob was her boyfriend. Then, I told her that I was also sensing the name Louis around her. The impression of a huckster came into my mind, and I expressed my feeling that Louis was an aggressive person always looking for an angle to acquire money.

After telling me that Louis was the name of her ex-husband, she described to me the difficult life that she had lived with him due to his get-rich-quick schemes.

Look what a lovely woman he gave up!

I told Janet when she sat down for a reading that I had the feeling of a large boat around her. Janet informed me that she had recently won a cruise for two, which would be going to the Caribbean. Her only problem was that she couldn't decide who she should invite to go with her. Should she invite her sister, Audrey, or her best friend, Veronica?

I thought of the nursery rhyme "Jack Sprat" and asked her who Jack was. Janet told me that Jack was her husband. It was then that she decided to invite Jack to go with her on the trip instead of Audrey or Veronica.

The poor guy didn't even make it onto her original short list!

When Albert walked into the room where the psychic fair was being held, he was wearing a full-face, feathered mask. To me, he almost looked as though he belonged in a carnival. He did not remove the mask even though it was inappropriate attire for where he was.

I let him speak first. He told me that he was on the way to a party but was anxious to have a psychic reading. He told me that he was embarrassed to be dressed like that because he always considered himself the strong, silent type.

I told Albert I was hearing the name Shelly. He identified her as the hostess of the party he was going to and then told me that he had met her on a blind date set up by his best friend.

A picture of a billiards parlor came into my mind and I told him that this was relevant in regard to Shelly and himself. He said that he took her to play billiards on their first date.

I'm sensing that there wouldn't have been a second date if he had wore the full–face, feathered mask on their first date!

The feeling that I got from Howie after meeting him for a reading was that he was emotionally detached but wanted a female companion. I asked him about the woman whose name started with an L. He eagerly explained to me that his best friend was arranging a blind date for him with a woman by the name of Laura.

Sports, games and competition came into my psychic vision and when I questioned Howie about them, he proudly admitted to me that he was training for the Olympic Games.

An uneasiness followed, suggesting to me that there was fighting and arguing surrounding him. Howie then admitted that his former girlfriend owed him money for unpaid utility bills and her portion of the rent.

It's not smart to get into a fight with someone training for the Olympics!

Keith walked into the room and then over to me for a reading. I immediately knew that this was going to be a complicated story. This is where more than one of my psychic senses usually kick in.

I asked Keith if he had gotten married on his birthday. He told me that I was correct. I then asked who Sandy was and he guiltily admitted to me that she was a former girlfriend. I continued, telling him that I was feeling someone named Hannah in his life. He acknowledged her as his wife. For some strange reason, I had the feeling that he wouldn't have met Hannah if it weren't for Sandy. He nodded his head "yes," telling me that I was correct in my reading so far.

I closed my eyes and saw in my psychic vision a jewelry shop, about which I quickly told Keith. "You're on the right track," he said while laughing. He told me that when he had gone to purchase an engagement ring for Sandy, Hannah was the salesgirl in the store. She was very patient and nice as a salesperson and suddenly, he had felt that he was in love with her. With this thought in mind, he then decided that he would buy Sandy only a string of pearls. He asked Hannah for her phone number and after dating her for just a few months, decided that Hannah was going to be the girl he would marry, and he did just that on his birthday.

Boy, they were certainly all connected!

I was feeling a birthday, hearing music and seeing writing when Marylou sat down for a reading. She smiled broadly and admitted to me that on her twenty-first birthday, she had received a piano from her boyfriend. She had already written her first song.

When I asked her why I was feeling wind and water, she said that she was planning to buy a sailboat for her boyfriend on his birthday.

Nice gifts. Maybe I should tell her when my birthday is!

Sid was what I would call a *serial seducer.* After meeting him for the first time at a psychic fair, I asked him who the woman was whose name began with an E. Sid identified the woman as a girlfriend named Ellen. He told me that he wasn't able to get where he wanted to in the relationship with her and referred to Ellen as the "smart one."

I felt that Sid was capable of being involved in many relationships at one time. After I expressed this feeling to him and said that he could commit the meanest of actions without feeling any guilt or shame, he smiled, looked proudly into my eyes and said, "Yes, I can."

Some claim to fame that is!

Herb was anxious for a reading at the fair and was probably sorry that he picked me to do it. I expressed to him that he needed to spend less and earn more. Herb agreed and admitted to me that he had to get some money into his wallet.

I told him I heard the name Mandy, at which he shook his head in disbelief. He then told me that she was his sweetheart. I explained to him that he didn't need to show his love for Mandy by spending his hard-earned money on fancy meals and expensive gifts when a simple kiss could show how he felt about her.

After suggesting to Herb that I sensed a positive change in fortune would take place soon, he informed me that he also believed that he was going to reach the top rung of his profession.

The following month, Herb called to tell me that he had been given the corner office.

Windows on two walls. Good for him!

Karen walked towards me for a reading, giving me the feeling that she had no fear of anyone or anything in her life. The clothing she wore reminded me of a Mardi Gras celebration.

I told her that I felt that she was playing "bridal hockey" with two young men. Karen admitted to me that she was currently engaged to two guys at the same time.

I asked her who Billy was. She told me that Billy was the name of both fiancés. Karen told me that she lived with her parents, who were always very supportive of her both financially and emotionally. It had become a very difficult situation because when one of the Billys called, her parents didn't know which Billy he was. She said that she was confused because she was in love with both of them.

I informed her that her love life was going to become even more complicated because there would be a new man coming into her life shortly. But, I assured her that she needn't worry because his name wasn't Billy.

I forgot to notice whether she was wearing two rings!

Tom sat down for his first psychic reading ever and I smelled flowers that he had recently sent to someone. He nodded his head, indicating that I was correct. I asked him who Caroline was and he informed me that she was his girlfriend and the recipient of the recently delivered bouquet.

I suggested to Tom that Caroline needed to avoid spending on impulse. My psychic vision was showing credit cards that were maxed out. She was definitely a person who believed in buying now and paying later. Tom was smiling at the fact that I had ascertained his girlfriend's weakness.

I asked Tom if his grandparents lived in his neighborhood. He confirmed that they lived directly across the street.

My psychic hearing was telling me that Tom held down two jobs, though one had nothing to do with the other. I asked him if he was a teacher of hip-hop dancing and a school bus driver. He said I was correct.

He was going to need five jobs if he married Caroline!

Lydia called for a first-time reading. I saw in my mind's eye a big dollar sign around a man in her life. When I asked Lydia who Jeremy was, she identified him as her multimillionaire boyfriend. I was feeling a huge age difference between the two of them. Lydia told me that Jeremy was old enough to be her grandfather.

I then sensed a teenage girl named Patricia who was threatening other students in her class. Lydia told me that her daughter, Patricia, was the school bully. The principal was constantly calling Lydia in for meetings regarding this problem.

I also sensed that there was a man named Todd in Patricia's life. I had a psychic vision of wedding bells around him. Lydia told me that Todd was her ex-husband and her daughter's father. Todd had just announced his engagement the previous weekend.

I was also being psychically told that Lydia was searching for love with no success. She told me that she used Jeremy for his money and that he really didn't make her happy. She also admitted to me that there was just no chemistry between them on her part.

Sometimes, you just can't have it all!

Larry called me on the phone sounding very upset. He told me that the situation in which he found himself required a lot of personal sacrifice. He claimed that I would never be able to figure out what his dilemma was.

Before he said anything further, I told Larry that I felt that there was infidelity in his family but not with him, his wife, his son or his daughter. My senses were informing me that his children's spouses were having an affair with each other. I was also feeling that Larry had grandchildren from both of his children's marriages, which only made the circumstances even more complicated.

There was silence on the line, causing me to think that the call had been disconnected. Finally, Larry asked, "Did someone else phone you and tell you this story about my family?"

"No," I answered. "I am seeing in my mind's eye that your son-in-law is having an affair with your daughter-in-law." I then told Larry that there was a lot of dishonesty and sneaky behavior taking place without his children knowing about it.

I would like to be a fly on the wall at their next Thanksgiving Day dinner!

Chapter Twelve

A Little Something Extra to Think About

Before caller ID came into our lives, nine out of ten times I would answer the telephone already knowing who the call was from, even if I hadn't heard from him or her in years. I would answer by saying the name of the person on the other end of the line. The caller would scream in delight.

Hi there!

It was the annual Christmas party given by a Wall Street brokerage firm. My intuitive powers happened to be acute at this particular time.

Steven sat down for a reading. I anticipated my client's imminent demise, and I don't mean physically. He was wearing a hat even though we were indoors and I knew exactly what he was going to say to me.

He started the session by making up stories to confuse me. I thought he was quite a character. I have been in this business professionally for over four decades and every day is devoted to some form of metaphysics. The last thing that someone should try to do is confuse a psychic. We have all devoted our lives to this calling. If a real psychic can't tell a phony, then no one can.

I have almost always gotten answers to every question. If I don't get an answer, then I know the incident or the person doesn't exist.

So, I sent Steven on his way and told him not to waste his or my time with his silly, made-up stories.

Just because you don't believe in it doesn't mean it's nonexistent!

When Joe sat down, I saw in my psychic vision an image from a particular television show. I wondered why I had received an impression of that specific sitcom.

It didn't take long for me to figure it out, though. Joe smiled and pointed to a water bottle on the table and asked me to shift it from one end of the table to the other. He wanted the container to move through my spiritual assertion. I guess he thought that if I twitched my nose, it would induce some type of action on the part of the plastic vessel which held my favorite beverage of H2O.

I told him that I was not capable of doing that. I could move it physically, but not psychically. He was not happy with that answer and emphatically implored me to use my "magic powers" to transport the bottle, even if it was just two inches from its original spot. I reiterated that I was not able to do transference tricks and perhaps he should go to a magician.

Sounds like someone is watching too much TV!

I met Chuck during a psychic party. He wasn't interested in having a reading. Instead, he asked me to teach him how to flirt. Chuck was what I would consider a very good-looking man, but very shy. He was unable even to make eye contact with me. We practiced role playing together.

The following month, Chuck telephoned me to say that he had finally mustered up the courage to invite a girl on a date, and she accepted.

Mission accomplished!

One of my steady clients paid me to fly out to Las Vegas in order to select the slot machines that were going to hit the jackpot. She paid for all my expenses and my hotel room.

I don't know whether it was me or just plain good fortune but for some reason, I picked the correct machines without the help of any psychic messages. It's different when you are playing casino games for someone else than when you are playing for yourself.

Talk about lucky guesses!

I received a phone call from a client who requested that I do a house party for her, which would involve many of her widowed women friends. Each of the women desired to be put in contact with her deceased spouse.

I knew that this would be an endeavor that would require tremendous concentration and meditation on my part, but I agreed to do what she requested.

I arrived early and found a houseful of excited ladies who were anticipating a day to remember. They were all waiting for the moment of psychic reunion with the men they had married many years earlier.

One by one, each woman came into the room, some clutching items belonging to their dearly departed mates. I knew that the expectations would be enormous, but I also hoped that if I handled the readings carefully, no one would be disappointed.

The afternoon was unfolding quite smoothly, and the women seemed thrilled with the outcome. It was a full and exhausting day for me, but well worth it after seeing the happy smiles on the faces of these widows.

I was almost through with all of my readings when I encountered a problem with one of the guests who had very recently lost her spouse. Her husband did not come to speak with her through me no matter how hard I tried. Various other individuals she knew came through, but not him. She became very upset and said that it was my fault or that he just didn't want to come through, which to her was very hurtful.

I explained to her that I was not in control of any of the entities who showed themselves to me. I do not choose which individual spirit will present itself. I certainly didn't wish to impose any anguish or disappointment. She did not accept this answer and became angry and offensive.

I could understand her emotional pain, but it wasn't me who caused it!

I received a phone call from a woman named Joan who had gotten my name and telephone number from one of her family members. This relative was a client of mine. Joan started her story by telling me that her husband, Bill, had died just days prior to her reaching out to me. She was not a believer in metaphysics and was skeptical regarding the following incident.

Joan told me that she owned a home computer, which she used to go on the Internet and send e-mails. She and her husband had individual e-mail addresses—a somewhat common practice among couples. Joan told me about an e-mail she had received from Bill two days after he had passed on.

The message, which Joan had read, told her that Bill was fine, that she was loved and that he missed her. It seemed that someone was signing on to a computer using her husband's e-mail password, which was personal information. Joan told me that Bill never would have disclosed that secret. He was a very private person.

Joan wanted to know what I thought. I asked her if she saved the e-mail. She told me that she tried, but for some reason couldn't. It just would not be saved. Could it be that it was a sadistic trick that someone was playing on her?

The fact that she could not save it gave me pause. Maybe it was her husband trying to contact her. This was the only reason I could think of for why it could not be saved. It's a story for many to ponder.

What do you think?

A Little Something Extra to Think About

Lara was a preteen girl who came to me for a reading at a psychic fair. She was wearing a see-through tube top, which was certainly getting the attention of all the fair goers.

When I asked her what was on her mind, she told me that shopping, fashion and being an attractive sex object for boys was what she needed to know about.

Although I am rarely shocked by young people, this teenage girl left me reeling. She was the epitome of an evolving culture that has taken over our society. Influenced by the media, corporate marketing and those individuals who are idolized by the youth of today, this young woman had no real role model to follow. She was a victim of a society that was showing her that she didn't have to be authentic or unique in her thinking or actions. She, along with countless other vulnerable youngsters, was being manipulated by teen magazines, television shows and Hollywood movies.

I urged her not to be a follower. I said that popularity was not as important as being genuine and sincere to oneself.

Several months later, she came back to me dressed more appropriately for her age. She told me that she had heard what I had said and that she was much happier now that she did not put pressure on herself to find a boy who would think she was just an object and not a person with real feelings.

Motivation must come from within. You have to believe it in order to make it work!

When Jim came to my table at a fair, I noticed how carefree and lighthearted he seemed to be. For this reason, I was slightly surprised when he asked me how long he was going to live and what the cause of his death would be.

I studied Jim's smiling face and noticed that he had become a little nervous after asking the question. Then, the smile vanished and a serious, pensive look began to appear on his handsome face.

"Why do you ask such a question?" I asked. "You are young and hopeful. Stay that way."

Jim looked at me with a thoughtful gaze and then replied with a typical answer that I have heard many times over the years from young adults in his age group. "I want to go bungee jumping, sky diving and all of that kind of stuff. If I know that I will live a long life, then I can do anything I want and not be afraid of dying young. By the way, I also want to know if I am going to die rich."

"Well, Jim," I answered, "first, let me tell you that I don't know everything, but I do know that you must make wise decisions regarding your life's experiences. You should not take foolish chances nor worry about how rich you will be when you die. It's not important how much money you have when you leave here. The thing that is truly significant is how many lives you have touched in a positive way."

Could I have told Jim the answer to his question regarding his time of passing? Maybe or maybe not, but why would anyone in good health—or, for that matter, in bad health—wish to know his hour of death?

Libby requested a reading with me at a psychic fair. At that moment in time, she was a student at a performing arts school. She wished to become an actress.

I told her that I understood her choice of vocation but I saw in my psychic vision a picture of her becoming a chef instead. I knew she had culinary skills.

Years later, I received a telephone call from Libby, who told me that she had quit acting school, attended culinary school and was now a chef who owned a restaurant.

She then asked if I would work as the entertainment in her restaurant. Libby felt that I could attract customers. I told her that I was flattered by her request but was totally overwhelmed with my own clientele.

She wanted to provide her customers with food for the mouth while I provided them with food for the soul!

I had never done a reading for Andrea before but she was anxious to try one after her friend Dorothy had enthusiastically recommended me to her. So, when Andrea called me for the phone reading, I asked her the usual question: "What would you like to know about?"

She answered, "Tell me everything about my husband."

I closed my eyes, meditated and got nothing in response. I decided to shuffle the cards, thinking that maybe I would get more information than a non-tarot reading. Still, I felt nothing.

So, with a little embarrassment, I replied, "I'm sorry, but I'm not getting anything regarding your husband."

Andrea answered, "That's because I don't have a husband. I want you to inform me about the man I'm going to marry eventually." She continued, telling me that she was curious about his name, birth date, height, weight, hair color, eye color and occupation. I told Andrea that I wasn't sensing any information regarding a husband and if I was, I would only be able to tell her when and how she would meet her future spouse.

Disappointed by my answer, she asked me to speak with her sister, Debbie, who was sitting next to her, which I did. Upon taking the phone, Debbie requested the same information that her sister had just asked me. "Tell me about my husband."

Thinking that Debbie was married and that I could maybe find some definitive information about her husband, I did my standard routine of obtaining information through meditation. Disappointedly, as before, when I did the same for her sister's reading, I received no psychic information.

When I relayed this news to Debbie, she told me that she, like her sister, didn't have a husband. She gave the telephone back to Andrea.

In obvious frustration, I said to Andrea, "If I wasn't able to get your information regarding your future husband, why did you think that I would be able to obtain information for your sister on the same subject, and in the same situation? Let's talk about real things that come up in your life and not what will possibly happen."

Fortunately, there was plenty for me to tell Andrea regarding what was going on in her life. She was quite thrilled with her reading even though it didn't include her matrimonial plans.

This was a lesson in futility. As good a psychic as I am, I am still a mortal. My anonymous source is the one of whom we should be in awe!

I call this story "Too Good to Be True."

I left my home early to work at a private party. Upon arriving at Bonnie's home, I sensed that all of the guests were very excited to be there. There were approximately thirty people from many different age groups at this gathering.

Bonnie led me down the steps to the furnished basement where there would be privacy while I did the readings. Before she left to go back upstairs, I thanked her for allowing me to use her home for this event and then requested that she send down the first guest to be read.

I began the day's activities and everything was moving along very smoothly. Happily, I was doing quite well with the readings and everyone appeared to be enjoying a metaphysical happening.

After doing a number of the readings, my next client, whose name was Claudia, came down to the basement. I waited patiently for her to relax and get into the moment.

Then, we started the reading. My accuracy seemed to frighten her, and she asked if I were a magician. She wanted to know how my tricks were done. She informed me that my answers were just too accurate and that I must have had a source who informed me about her life. She was sure that I had spoken with her mother and she had filled me in on all the details.

I explained to Claudia that I had the gift of clairvoyance and received messages from a source outside of our reality. I assured her that I had never met her or her mother and that I didn't even know her last name or where she or her family lived.

Claudia was adamant in her distrust. She stood up from her chair and hurried up the steps to announce to everyone that I was a fraud. Bonnie was shocked at the accusation and advised Claudia and the remaining guests that I hadn't even asked for a list of names in advance of the party.

But Claudia's mind was not going to be changed. She was sure that I had gotten all her personal information from the hostess or off of a Web site because the reading was just too perfect—a multitude of details were correct. She then remarked that she was afraid of me and that this was a total scam.

The party abruptly ended. I left early because I certainly didn't want anyone to feel uncomfortable.

The following week, Bonnie called me on the telephone and asked that I return to her home to do more readings for her other friends who hadn't gotten one because of my hasty departure. She promised that Claudia would not be present and then apologized to me for the behavior of her guest the previous week.

I was criticized for being too good. Claudia should know that this wasn't the only time I was accused of that!

A Little Something Extra to Think About

When Mary sat down for a reading, I felt that she was very fearful. I asked her if she was frightened to be at home by herself. She confirmed this by telling me that she was very afraid because her house was haunted.

Mary asked me if I would come to her house to perform a ceremony to rid her residence of ghosts. I declined her request, so she reached into her purse and brought out a picture that showed her posed in the middle of her kitchen. She asked me if I could see the ghosts standing next to her. After carefully scrutinizing the photograph, I confessed that the only thing visible to me was Mary leaning on the refrigerator.

Then, Mary, with an attitude of obvious disgust, got up from the table and told me that she was going to find another psychic with "super powers" to help her with the problem in her house. I wished her luck in her pursuit of the apparitions and suggested that she sell the home she was currently living in and then possibly find a new one that was more comfortable for her to occupy.

Maybe the ghosts were there or maybe not. I know that I didn't see them!

THE END…?

Living Our Lives

Now, after reading my book, you are probably feeling one of two mindsets. Either you are cynical, and therefore saying, "There is no way that this woman can know what she knows, and how come she can get these messages and I can't? It's all a sham. I've heard and read about these things."

Or, perhaps on the positive side, maybe you are pondering in your mind, Well if she can do it, why can't I? Joy says everyone has some type of ability and maybe I am just overlooking it.

There might even be a third scenario. You might be saying to yourself, "I think that I remember having a psychic moment when…"

This last one is probably the most realistic. You can believe it or not, but each of you has had psychic experiences, whether it was an odd coincidence, an accurate feeling about something or a dream that came true even though it seemed an impossibility.

For those of you who are naysayers, I implore you not to be afraid of this phenomenon. Instinct is a natural ability with which we have all been endowed. You can deny its existence, but denial doesn't mean that this gift is not a prevalent trait in all of our minds and lives.

For those who are fervent believers in metaphysics, please don't let anyone try to tell you that you don't know what you are talking about. Just keep your mind clear, your senses alert and your attitude positive, and you will see that this talent might start to show itself, if it hasn't already done so. Learn to meditate and it will free your mind of the mundane problems you face every day.

I say to all skeptics, enthusiasts and those who aren't sure of how they feel on the subject to just keep an open attitude and trust your intuition because a buried treasure can possibly reveal itself in your psyche. Be ready because it is coming, but only when you allow it to.

Trust that little voice you hear and embrace the quick, sudden vision that you see. Consider the vaguely remembered fragrance you inhale, feel the familiarity of a simple object when you touch it and enjoy the taste of that recollection from another era in your life. They are all telling you to believe in yourself and your feelings. Through these senses, you will be led to the truth about your abilities!

See, didn't I tell you that you would enjoy this book? Bye now. I will be thinking about you…

Afterword by Natalie Krous

From the time I first met Joy, I was astounded by her psychic ability. As the years moved forward and we became good friends, the astonishment never abated. It is for this reason that I suggested we write a book together. Believing that such a gifted talent should not go undocumented, I truly consider myself the lucky one who was chosen by destiny to record it. Joy is the eighth wonder of the world—finally marked and unearthed.

www.ingramcontent.com/pod-product-compliance
Lightning Source LLC
LaVergne TN
LVHW051038080426
835508LV00019B/1582